Principles in Practice

The Principles in Practice imprint offers teachers concrete illustrations of effective classroom practices based in NCTE research briefs and policy statements. Each book discusses the research on a specific topic, links the research to an NCTE brief or policy statement, and then demonstrates how those principles come alive in practice: by showcasing actual classroom practices that demonstrate the policies in action; by talking about research in practical, teacher-friendly language; and by offering teachers possibilities for rethinking their own practices in light of the ideas presented in the books. Books within the imprint are grouped in strands, each strand focused on a significant topic of interest.

Volumes in the Adolescent Literacy Strand

Adolescent Literacy at Risk? The Impact of Standards (2009) Rebecca Bowers Sipe

Adolescents and Digital Literacies: Learning Alongside Our Students (2010) Sara Kajder

Adolescent Literacy and the Teaching of Reading: Lessons for Teachers of Literature (2010) Deborah Appleman

Volumes in the Writing in Today's Classrooms Strand

Writing in the Dialogical Classroom: Students and Teachers Responding to the Texts of Their Lives (2011) Bob Fecho

Becoming Writers in the Elementary Classroom: Visions and Decisions (2011) Katie Van Sluys

Writing Instruction in the Culturally Relevant Classroom (2011) Maisha T. Winn and Latrise P. Johnson

Volumes in the Literacy Assessment Strand

Our Better Judgment: Teacher Leadership for Writing Assessment (2012) Chris W. Gallagher and Eric D. Turley

Beyond Standardized Truth: Improving Teaching and Learning through Inquiry-Based Reading Assessment (2012) Scott Filkins

Beyond Standardized Truth

Improving Teaching and Learning through Inquiry-Based Reading Assessment

Scott Filkins

Champaign (Illinois) Unit 4 Schools

National Council of Teachers of English
1111 W. Kenyon Road, Urbana, Illinois 61801-1096

All author proceeds for this book will be donated in honor of the memory of Clif Aldridge to the Clif Rocks! fund, supporting scholarships at Champaign Centennial High School, the Illinois State University chapter of Sigma Chi Fraternity, and the needs of cancer patients between the ages of eighteen and twenty-three at Carle and Provena Covenant Hospitals.

Staff Editor: Bonny Graham

Imprint Editor: Cathy Fleischer

Interior Design: Victoria Pohlmann

Cover Design: Pat Mayer

Cover Photo: Thompson-McClellan

NCTE Stock Number: 02916

Library of Congress Cataloging-in-Publication Data

Filkins, Scott R.
    Beyond standardized truth : improving teaching and learning through inquiry-based reading assessment / Scott R. Filkins.
          p. cm.
    Includes biliographical references and index.
    ISBN 978-0-8141-0291-6 ((pbk))
  1. Reading—Ability testing—United States. 2. Education—Standards—United States. I. Title.
    LB1050.46.F48 2012
    379.1'510973—dc23
                                                                   2012021155

For Joan Wagner Filkins, who taught me to read,
and Colin James Filkins, who allowed me to pay the favor forward.

Contents

Acknowledgments . . . . **ix**

Excerpts from the IRA–NCTE *Standards for the Assessment of Reading and Writing*, Revised Edition. . . **xi**

Chapter 1 . . . . Confessions of an Unprincipled Reading Assessor 1

Chapter 2 . . . . Seeking Truth, Considering Consequences: Getting into Students' Heads through Inquiry-Based Assessment. 18

Chapter 3 . . . . Formative Reading Assessment in Action 52

Chapter 4 . . . . Beyond "Zenning It": Reflecting on Professional Practice through Reading Assessment. 80

Chapter 5 . . . . Improving Assessment through Caring, Collaboration, and Collective Responsibility 103

Annotated Bibliography 123

Works Cited 127

Index. 129

Author. 133

Acknowledgments

As I finish this project, I'm reminded of Edith Wharton's recollection of her attempt to write her first book, *The House of Mirth*. "I don't yet know how to write a novel," she recalled, "but I know how to find out how to."

I'm indebted to the following people for the roles they played in the rewarding process of "finding out" how to write a book about secondary reading assessment:

- Will, Chris, Kathy, Liz, Nikki, Gary, Stephanie, and Faith—the eight Central High School teachers who let me into their classrooms for discovery and collaboration, plied only with pasta, wine, and a free clipboard;

- The students and their families who graciously allowed me to include their work in this volume;

- The teachers at Champaign's two high schools, for their dedication to their craft and for their friendship across the years;

- Joe Williams and Judy Wiegand, for allowing formative reading assessment to be my professional focus for a semester of work at Central;

- Patrick Berry and Charlie Weinberg, for reading the first written artifact associated with this project, a nearly incomprehensible proposal they both responded to with much more respect than it deserved;

- Greg Johnson and Ryan Cowell, for reading early and later drafts with critical care, and for being part of the work and talk that undergirded this project;

- The many teachers affiliated with the University of Illinois Writing Project (especially our director, Libbie Morley), for their enthusiasm for writing, professional development, and excellent snacks;

- The University of Illinois faculty who have given me so many new ways to think about my students and my practice, particularly Catherine Prendergast, Paul Prior, Mark Dressman, Sarah McCarthey, Gail Hawisher, and Anne Haas Dyson;

- The educators who read an earlier draft of this book through the NCTE Books Program review process, for their combination of supportive enthusiasm and critical suggestions for improvement;

- Kurt Austin and Bonny Graham, for their extraordinary attention to detail and patience with my lack thereof; and

- Cathy Fleischer, a true mentor.

Standards for the Assessment of Reading and Writing, Revised Edition

A publication of the IRA–NCTE Joint Task Force on Assessment

Introduction

This document provides a set of standards to guide decisions about assessing the teaching and learning of literacy. In the past 30 years, research has produced revolutionary changes in our understanding of language, learning, and the complex literacy demands of our rapidly changing society. The standards proposed in this document are intended to reflect these advances in our understanding.

Readers of this document most likely share common experiences with respect to literacy and assessment. For example, in our own school days, we were directed to read to get the correct meaning of a text so that we could answer questions put to us by someone who already knew that correct meaning or by a test (often multiple choice) for which the correct answers were already determined. In order to develop assessment practices that serve students in an increasingly complex society, we must outgrow the limitations of our own schooling histories and understand language, literacy, and assessment in more complex ways. Literacy involves not just reading and writing, but a wide range of related language activities. It is both more social and more personal than a mere set of skills.

The need to understand language is particularly important. Language is not only the object of assessment but also part of the process of assessment. Consequently, any discussion of literacy assessment must include a discussion of language—what it is, how it is learned, and how it relates to assessment. Before we state our assessment standards, then, we will give an overview of what we mean by assessment and how we understand language and its relationship to assessment.

The Nature of Assessment

For many years, a transmission view of knowledge, curriculum, and assessment dominated and appeared to satisfy our social, political, and economic needs. Knowledge was regarded as a static entity that was "out there" somewhere, so the key educational question was, How do you get it from out there into students' heads? The corollary assessment question was, What counts as evidence that the knowledge really is in their heads? In a transmission view, it made sense to develop educational standards that specified the content of instruction before developing assessment procedures and engagements.

In the 1920s, notions of the basic purposes of schooling began to shift from an emphasis on the transmission of knowledge to the more complex nurturing of independent and collaborative learning and of problem solving. This shift has gained increasing prominence in today's postindustrial society, with its ever-expanding need for workers with strong communication skills and dispositions toward problem solving and collaborating. A curriculum committed to independent learning is built on the premise that inquiry, rather than mere transmission of knowledge, is the basis of teaching and learning.

Standards for the Assessment of Reading and Writing

This shift from knowledge transmission to inquiry as a primary goal of schools has important implications for assessment. In a knowledge-transmission framework, tests of static knowledge can suffice as assessment instruments. Students are the participants who are primarily accountable (either they have the knowledge or they don't), with teachers held accountable next. Policymakers, including school board members, trustees, or regents, are the primary recipients of assessment data. An inquiry framework changes the role of assessment and the roles of the participants. Within this framework, assessment is the exploration of how the educational environment and the participants in the educational community support the process of students as they learn to become independent and collaborative thinkers and problem solvers. This exploration includes an examination of the environment for teaching and learning, the processes and products of learning, and the degree to which all participants—students, teachers, administrators, parents, and board members—meet their obligation to support inquiry. Such assessments examine not only learning over time but also the contexts of learning.

Inquiry emphasizes different processes and types of knowledge than does knowledge transmission. For example, it values the ability to recognize problems and to generate multiple and diverse perspectives in trying to solve them. An inquiry stance asserts that while knowledge and language are likely to change over time, the need for learners at all levels (students, teachers, parents, administrators, and policymakers) who can solve new problems, generate new knowledge, and invent new language practices will remain constant. An inquiry perspective promotes problem posing and problem solving as goals for all participants in the educational community. For example, inquiry values the question of how information from different sources can be used to solve a particular problem. It values explorations of how teachers can promote critical thinking for all students. And it raises the question of why our society privileges the knowledge and cultural heritage of some groups over others within current school settings.

Inquiry fits the needs of a multicultural society in which it is essential to value and find strength in cultural diversity. It also honors the commitment to raising questions and generating multiple solutions. Various stakeholders and cultural groups provide different answers and new perspectives on problems. Respecting difference among learners enriches the curriculum and reduces the likelihood of problematic curricular narrowing.

Just as the principle of inquiry values difference, so the principle of difference values conversation over recitation as the primary mode of discourse. In a recitation, it is assumed that one person, the teacher, possesses the answers and that the others, the students, interact with the teacher and one another in an attempt to uncover the teacher's knowledge. In a conversation, all of the stakeholders in the educational environment (students, parents, teachers, specialists, administrators, and policymakers) have a voice at the table as curriculum, standards, and assessments are negotiated. Neither inquiry nor learning is viewed as the exclusive domain of students and teachers; both are primary concerns for all members of the school community. For example, administrators ask themselves hard questions about whether the structures they have established support staff development, teacher reflection, and student learning. School board members ask themselves whether they have lived up to

Standards for the Assessment of Reading and Writing

the standards they have set for themselves and their schools to provide teachers and students with the resources they need to guarantee learning opportunities.

Quality assessment, then, hinges on the process of setting up conditions so that the classroom, the school, and the community become centers of inquiry where students, teachers, and other members of the school community investigate their own learning, both individually and collaboratively. The onus of assessment does not fall disproportionately upon students and teachers (which is often the case in schools today); instead, all those inquiring into the nature and effectiveness of educational practices are responsible for investigating the roles they have played. Different members of the school community have different but interacting interests, roles, and responsibilities, and assessment is the medium that allows all to explore what they have learned and whether they have met their responsibilities to the school community.

The Nature of Language

Language is very much like a living organism. It cannot be put together from parts like a machine, and it is constantly changing. Like a living organism, it exists only in interaction with others, in a social interdependence. Language is a system of signs through and within which we represent and make sense of the world and of ourselves. Language does not contain meaning; rather, meaning is constructed in the social relationships within which language is used. Individuals make sense of language within their social relationships, their personal histories, and their collective memory. In order to make sense of even a single word, people take into account the situation and their relationship with the speaker or writer.

Take, for example, *family*, a word often used as if all members of society agree on its meaning. The word may mean different things in different contexts, however, whether cultural, situational, or personal. To a middle-aged white person whose parents moved across country with their two children and who repeated that experience herself, *family* may mean the nuclear family structure in which she grew up and in which she is raising her own children. To someone from a different culture—perhaps an African American or Asian American—the word may conjure images of the constellation of grandparents, aunts, uncles, and cousins who live together or near one another. So, meaning may vary from one person to another, as in this case, where meanings attached to the word *family* are likely to differ depending on one's own experience in the family or families one has lived with. Thus, individuals make different sense of apparently similar language to the extent that their cultural and personal histories do not coincide. Consequently, when we attempt to standardize a test (by making it the same for everyone), we make the tenuous assumption that students will all make the same meaning from the language of our instructions and the language of the individual items.

Different cultures also have different ways of representing the world, themselves, and their intentions with language. For example, in any given cultural group, people have different ways of greeting one another, depending on the situation (e.g., a business meeting, a funeral, a date) and on their relationship to each other. Our own language practices come from our cultural experience, but they are also part of the collective practice that forms the

Standards for the Assessment of Reading and Writing

culture. Indeed, the different ways people use language to make sense of the world and of their lives are the major distinguishing features of different cultural groups.

At the same time, language is always changing as we use it. Words acquire different meanings, and new language structures and uses appear as people stretch and pull the language to make new meanings. Consequently, the meaning that individuals make from language varies across time, social situation, personal perspective, and cultural group.

The Nature of Literacy

The nature of literacy is also continually changing. Today, many children read more online than offline. They are growing into a digital world in which relatively little reading and writing involves paper, most reading and writing involves images as much as print, and writing (both formal and less formal, the latter including e-mail, texts, Facebook posts, etc.) is becoming equal to, or even supplanting, reading as a primary literacy engagement. The tools of literacy are changing rapidly as new forms of Internet communication technology (ICT) are created, including (at the time of writing) bulletin boards, Web editors, blogs, virtual worlds, and social networking sites such as Ning and MySpace. The social practices of literacy also change as a result of using digital technologies, as does the development of language. New literate practices are learned and refined just by existing from day to day in what has become known as the mediasphere. For example, living with cell phones leads to texting, which changes how people view writing and how they write, and frequenting Web 2.0 sites, such as the video-sharing service YouTube, privileges a visual mode and shapes both attention to and facility with other modes of meaning making. The literacies children encounter by the end of their schooling were unimagined when they began.

Reading and writing online changes what it means to read, write, and comprehend. Literacy practices now involve both the creation and use of multimodal texts (broadly defined). Creating multimodal texts requires knowing the properties and limitations of different digital tools so that decisions can be made about how best to serve one's intentions. Participating in social networking sites, for example, requires new literacy practices; new literacy practices shape how users are perceived and how they construct identities. This leads to new areas needing to be assessed, including how youths create and enhance multiple identities using digital tools and virtual spaces. We now need to be concerned with teaching and assessing how students take an idea in print and represent it with video clips for other audiences. Similarly, we must be concerned about the stances and practices involved in taking an idea presented in one modality (e.g., print) and transcribing or transmediating it into another (e.g., digital video), and we must consider what possibilities and limitations a particular mode offers and how that relates to its desirability over other modes for particular purposes and situations. Children use different comprehension strategies online and offline, and assessments of the two show different pictures of their literacy development. Online readers, by choosing hypertext and intertext links, actually construct the texts that they read as well as the meanings they make. New multimodal texts require new critical media literacies, linked to classical critical literacy notions of how media culture is created, appropriated, and subsequently colonizes the broader notions of culture—for example, how youth culture is defined by and used to define what youths do, what they buy, and with whom they associate.

Standards for the Assessment of Reading and Writing

The definitions of literacy that have dominated schooling and are insisted on by most current testing systems are inadequate for a new, highly networked information age. Failure to help all students acquire literacies for this age will not serve them or society well. Not to teach the necessary skills, strategies, dispositions, and social practices is to deny children full access to economic, social, and political participation in the new global society. Not to assess these capabilities will result in curricular neglect and a lack of information to inform instruction.

The Learning of Language

By the time children arrive at school, they have learned to speak at least one language and have mastered most of the language structures they will ever use. Through social interaction, using the language they hear around them from birth, they have developed, without their awareness, the underlying rules of grammar and the vocabulary that give meaning to the world as they see it. Nonetheless, we often teach language in schools as if children came to our classrooms with little or no language competence. Nothing could be further from the truth. Children can request, demand, explain, recount, persuade, and express opinions. They bring to school the ability to narrate their own life histories. They are authors creating meaning with language long before they arrive at school.

As children acquire language in social interaction, particularly with others whose language is different or more complex, they gain flexibility in using language for different purposes and in different social situations. Learning a second language or dialect roughly parallels learning the first, for learning any language also entails becoming competent in the social relationships that underlie it. Children also develop fluent use of language without explicit knowledge of or instruction in rules and grammars. This means that grammars and rules are taught most productively as tools for analyzing language after it has been acquired. Even adults who have considerable facility with the language frequently can articulate few, if any, grammar or language rules. In spite of this truism, we often go about assessment and instruction in schools as if this were not the case.

Furthermore, although we pretend otherwise, language is not acquired in any simple hierarchical sequence.

In some ways, school actually plays a modest role in language acquisition, the bulk of which occurs outside of school. In schools, we must learn to teach language in a way that preserves and respects individuality at the same time that we empower students to learn how to be responsible and responsive members of learning communities. In other words, we must respect their right to their own interpretations of language, including the texts they read and hear, but we must help them learn that meaning is negotiated with other members of the learning communities within which they live and work. To participate in that negotiation, they must understand and be able to master the language practices and means of negotiation of the cultures within which they live. They must understand the language conventions that are sanctioned in different social situations and the consequences of adhering to or violating those conventions.

Although much of our language is learned outside school, studying language is the foundation of all schooling, not just of the language arts. For example, in science class, we make knowledge of the world using language. To study science, then, we must study the language through which we make scientific knowledge, language that has an important impact on the curriculum. If in reading and writing about science the language is dispassionate and distancing, then that is part of the knowledge that students construct about science, part of the way they relate to the world through science.

The Assessment of Language

Our description of language and language learning has important implications for the assessment of language, first because it is the object of assessment (the thing being assessed) and second because it is the medium of assessment (the means through and within which we assess). Instructional outcomes in the language arts and assessment policies and practices should reflect what we know about language and its acquisition. For example, to base a test on the assumption that there is a single correct way to write a persuasive essay is a dubious practice. Persuading someone to buy a house is not the same as persuading someone to go on a date. Persuading someone in a less powerful position is not the same as persuading someone in a more powerful position—which is to say that persuasive practices differ across situations, purposes, and cultural groups. Similarly, that texts can (and should) be read from different perspectives must be taken as a certainty—a goal of schooling not to be disrupted by assessment practices that pretend otherwise. To assert through a multiple-choice test that a piece of text has only one meaning is unacceptable, given what we know of language.

Moreover, to the extent that assessment practices legitimize only the meanings and language practices of particular cultural groups, these practices are acts of cultural oppression. When our assessments give greater status to one kind of writing over another—for example, expository writing over narrative writing—we are making very powerful controlling statements about the legitimacy of particular ways of representing the world. These statements tend to be reflected in classroom practices.

When we attempt to document students' language development, we are partly involved in producing that development. For example, if we decide that certain skills are "basic" and some are "higher level," and that the former need to be acquired before the latter, that decision affects the way we organize classrooms, plan our teaching, group students, and discuss reading and writing with them. The way we teach literacy, the way we sequence lessons, the way we group students, even the way we physically arrange the classroom all have an impact on their learning.

The Language of Assessment

Because it involves language, assessment is an interpretive process. Just as we construct meanings for texts that we read and write, so do we construct "readings" or interpretations of our students based upon the many "texts" they provide for us. These assessment texts come in the form of the pieces that students write, their responses to literature, the various assignments and projects they complete, the contributions they make to discussions, their behavior in different settings, the questions they ask in the classroom or in conferences, their performances or demonstrations involving language use, and tests of their language competence. Two different people assessing a student's reading or writing, his or her literate development, may use different words to describe it.

Standards for the Assessment of Reading and Writing

In classrooms, teachers assess students' writing and reading and make evaluative comments about writers whose work is read. The language of this classroom assessment becomes the language of the literate classroom community and thus becomes the language through which students evaluate their own reading and writing. If the language of classroom assessment implies that there are several interpretations of any particular text, students will come to gain confidence as they assess their own interpretations and will value diversity in the classroom. If, on the other hand, the language of classroom assessment implies that reading and writing can be reduced to a simple continuum of quality, students will assess their own literacy only in terms of their place on that continuum relative to other students, without reflecting productively on their own reading and writing practices.

When teachers write report cards, they are faced with difficult language decisions. They must find words to represent a student's literate development in all its complexity, often within severe time, space, and format constraints. They must also accomplish this within the diverse relationships and cultural backgrounds among the parents, students, and administrators who might read the reports. Some teachers are faced with reducing extensive and complex knowledge about each student's development to a single word or letter. This situation confronts them with very difficult ethical dilemmas. Indeed, the greater the knowledge the teacher has of the student's literacy, the more difficult this task becomes.

But it is not just classroom assessment that is interpretive. The public "reads" students, teachers, and schools from the data that are provided. Parents make sense of a test score or a report card grade or comment based on their own schooling history, beliefs, and values. A test score may look "scientific" and "objective," but it too must be interpreted, which is always a subjective and value-laden process.

The terms with which people discuss students' literacy development have also changed over time. For example, in recent history, students considered to be having difficulty becoming literate have acquired different labels, such as *basic writer, remedial reader, disadvantaged, learning disabled, underachiever, struggling student,* or *retarded reader.* These different terms can have quite different consequences. Students described as "learning disabled" are often treated and taught quite differently from students who are similarly literate but described as "remedial readers."

Further, assessment itself is the object of much discussion, and the language of that discussion is also important. For example, teachers' observations are often described as informal and subjective and contrasted with test results that are considered "formal" and "objective." The knowledge constructed in a discussion that uses these terms would be quite different from that constructed in a discussion in which teachers' observations were described as "direct documentation" and test results as "indirect estimation."

Assessment terms change as different groups appropriate them for different purposes and as situations change. Recent discussions about assessment have changed some of the ways in which previously reasonably predictable words are used, belying the simplicity of the glossary we include at the end of this document. For example, the term *norm-referenced* once meant that assessment data on one student, typically test data, were interpreted in comparison with the data on other students who were considered similar. A norm-referenced interpretation of a student's writing might assert that it is "as good as that of 20 percent of

Standards for the Assessment of Reading and Writing

the students that age in the country." Similarly, the term *criterion-referenced assessment* once meant simply that a student's performance was interpreted with respect to a particular level of performance—either it met the criterion or it did not. Recently, however, it has become much less clear how these terms are being used. The line between criterion and norm has broken down. For example, *criterion* has recently come to mean "dimension" or "valued characteristic." *Norm* has come to be used in much the same sense. But even in the earlier (and still more common) meaning, most criteria for criterion-referenced tests are arrived at by finding out how a group of students performs on the test and then setting criteria in ac-cord with what seems a reasonable point for a student's passing or failing the test.

In other words, assessment is never merely a technical process. Assessment is always representational and interpretive because it involves representing children's development. Assessment practices shape the ways we see children, how they see themselves, and how they engage in future learning. Assessment is social and, because of its consequences, political. As with other such socially consequential practices, it is necessary to have standards against which practitioners can judge the responsibility of their practices.

Following are the summary paragraphs for all eleven standards. To read the expanded discussions and the case studies, see http://www.ncte.org/standards/assessmentstandards/introduction.

The Standards

1. The interests of the student are paramount in assessment.

Assessment experiences at all levels, whether formative or summative, have consequences for students (see standard 7). Assessments may alter their educational opportunities, increase or decrease their motivation to learn, elicit positive or negative feelings about themselves and others, and influence their understanding of what it means to be literate, educated, or suc-cessful. It is not enough for assessment to serve the well-being of students "on average"; we must aim for assessment to serve, not harm, each and every student.

2. The teacher is the most important agent of assessment.

Most educational assessment takes place in the classroom, as teachers and students interact with one another. Teachers design, assign, observe, collaborate in, and interpret the work of students in their classrooms. They assign meaning to interactions and evaluate the informa-tion that they receive and create in these settings. In short, teachers are the primary agents, not passive consumers, of assessment information. It is their ongoing, formative assessments that primarily influence students' learning. This standard acknowledges the critical role of the teacher and the consequences and responsibilities that accompany this role.

3. The primary purpose of assessment is to improve teaching and learning.

Assessment is used in educational settings for a variety of purposes, such as keeping track of learning, diagnosing reading and writing difficulties, determining eligibility for programs, evaluating programs, evaluating teaching, and reporting to others. Underlying all these purposes is a basic concern for improving teaching and learning. In the United States it is common to use testing for accountability, but the ultimate goal remains the improvement of teaching and learning. Similarly, we use assessments to determine eligibility for special education services, but the goal is more appropriate teaching and better learning for particular students. In both cases, if improved teaching and learning do not result, the assessment practices are not valid (see standard 7).

4. Assessment must reflect and allow for critical inquiry into curriculum and instruction.

Sound educational practices start with a curriculum that values complex literacy, instructional practices that nurture it, and assessments that fully reflect it. In order for assessment to allow productive inquiry into curriculum and instruction, it must reflect the complexity of that curriculum as well as the instructional practices in schools. This is particularly important because assessment shapes teaching, learning, and policy. Assessment that reflects an impoverished view of literacy will result in a diminished curriculum and distorted instruction and will not enable productive problem solving or instructional improvement. Because assessment shapes instruction, the higher the stakes of the assessment, the more important it is that it reflect this full complexity.

5. Assessment must recognize and reflect the intellectually and socially complex nature of reading and writing and the important roles of school, home, and society in literacy development.

Literacy is complex, social, and constantly changing. The literacies of students graduating from high school today were barely imaginable when they began their schooling. Outside of school, students live and will go on to work in a media culture with practices unlike those currently occurring in school (even in the setting of the school media center). Students need to acquire competencies with word processors, blogs, wikis, Web browsers, instant messaging, listservs, bulletin boards, virtual worlds, video editors, presentation software, and many other literate tools and practices.

Traditional, simple definitions of literacy will not help prepare students for the literate lives of the present—let alone the future. Consequently, reading and writing cannot usefully be assessed as a set of isolated, independent tasks or events. It is critical to gather specific information about materials, tasks, and media being used with students for both instructional and assessment purposes. In addition, we need to assess how practices are used to participate in the broader media culture as well as to examine how the broader culture assigns status to some practices over others (e.g., texting as contrasted to writing paragraph summaries in language arts class).

Whatever the medium, literacy is social and involves negotiations among authors and readers around meanings, purposes, and contexts. Literate practices are now rarely solitary cognitive acts. Furthermore, literate practices differ across social and cultural contexts and across different media. Students' behavior in one setting may not be at all representative of their behavior in another. This may be particularly true of English-language learners who may lack the fluency to express themselves fully inside the classroom but may be lively contributors in their families and communities.

Standards for the Assessment of Reading and Writing

6. Assessment must be fair and equitable.

We live in a multicultural society with laws that promise equal rights to all. Our school communities must work to ensure that all students, as different as they are in cultural, ethnic, religious, linguistic, and economic background, receive a fair and equitable education. Assessment plays an important part in ensuring fairness and equity, first, because it is intimately related to curriculum, instruction, and learning, and second, because assessment provides a seemingly impartial way of determining who should and who should not be given access to educational institutions and resources. To be fair, then, assessment must be as free as possible of biases based on ethnic group, gender, nationality, religion, socioeconomic condition, sexual orientation, or disability. Furthermore, assessment must help us to confront biases that exist in schooling.

7. The consequences of an assessment procedure are the first and most important consideration in establishing the validity of the assessment.

Tests, checklists, observation schedules, and other assessments cannot be evaluated out of the context of their use. If a perfectly reliable and comprehensive literacy test were designed but using it took three weeks away from children's learning and half the annual budget for instructional materials, we would have to weigh these consequences against any value gained from using the test. If its use resulted in teachers building a productive learning community around the data and making important changes in their instruction, we would also have to weigh these consequences. This standard essentially argues for "environmental impact" projections, along with careful, ongoing analyses of the consequences of assessment practices. Responsibility for this standard lies with the entire school community, to ensure that assessments are not used in ways that have negative consequences for schools and students. Any assessment procedure that does not contribute positively to teaching and learning should not be used.

8. The assessment process should involve multiple perspectives and sources of data.

Perfect assessments and perfect assessors do not exist. Every person involved in assessment is limited in his or her interpretation of the teaching and learning of reading and writing. Similarly, each text and each assessment procedure has its own limitations and biases. Although we cannot totally eliminate these biases and limitations from people or tests, we can try to ensure that they are held in balance and that all stakeholders are made aware of them. The more consequential the decision, the more important it is to seek diverse perspectives and independent sources of data. For example, decisions about placement in or eligibility for specialized programs have a profound influence on a student's life and learning. Such decisions are simply too important to make on the basis of a single measure, evaluation tool, or perspective.

9. Assessment must be based in the local school learning community, including active and essential participation of families and community members.

Standards for the Assessment of Reading and Writing

The teacher is the primary agent of assessment and the classroom is the location of the most important assessment practices, but the most effective assessment unit is the local school learning community. First, the collective experience and values of the community can offer a sounding board for innovation and multiple perspectives to provide depth of understanding and to counter individual and cultural biases. Second, the involvement of all parties in assessment encourages a cooperative, committed relationship among them rather than an adversarial one. Third, because language learning is not restricted to what occurs in school, assessment must go beyond the school curriculum.

The local school learning community is also a more appropriate foundation for assessment than larger units such as the school district, county, state, province, or country. These larger units do not offer the relational possibilities and commitments necessary for a learning community. The distance from the problems to be solved and among the participants reduces the probability of feelings of involvement and commitment and increases the possibility that assessment will become merely a means of placing blame.

10. All stakeholders in the educational community—students, families, teachers, administrators, policymakers, and the public—must have an equal voice in the development, interpretation, and reporting of assessment information.

Each of the constituents named in this standard has a stake in assessment. Students are concerned because their literacy learning, their concepts of themselves as literate people, and the quality of their subsequent lives and careers are at stake. Teachers have at stake their understandings of their students, their professional practice and knowledge, their perceptions of themselves as teachers, and the quality of their work life and standing in the community. Families clearly have an investment in their children's learning, well-being, and educational future. The public invests money in education, in part as an investment in the future, and has a stake in maintaining the quality of that investment. The stewardship of the investment involves administrators and policymakers. Assessment is always value laden, and the ongoing participation of all parties involved in it is necessary in a democratic society. When any one perspective is missing, silenced, or privileged above others, the assessment picture is distorted.

11. Families must be involved as active, essential participants in the assessment process.

In many schools, families stand on the periphery of the school community, some feeling hopeless, helpless, and unwanted. However, the more families understand their children's progress in school, the more they can contribute to that progress. If teachers are to understand how best to assist children from cultures that are different from their own, families are a particularly important resource. Families must become, and be helped to become, active participants in the assessment process.

For the complete Standards *document, see http://www.ncte.org/standards/assessmentstandards/ introduction or https://secure.ncte.org/store/assessment-standards-revised.*

Chapter One

Confessions of an Unprincipled Reading Assessor

I imagine that people in other professions have recurring dreams related to the shared fears and stresses of their work, but I like to think that the nightmares teachers have are especially telling of our daily anxieties.

As an undergraduate in teacher education, for example, I'd occasionally have the dream in which I showed up to a lecture hall for a final exam, only to realize that I'd never attended the class or done any of the readings in preparation for it. I'm happy to say that this dream, rooted in my persistent fear of being caught underprepared, never happened in real life.

When I began teaching high school English in 1998, the setting and specifics of this dream changed, but the anxiety fueling it did not. Around late July, I'd start having dreams of arriving to teach a class in which not a single student was familiar. I'd have no idea of the focus of the course, not to mention the plan for the period that had just begun. Unlike the dream from undergraduate days, variations of this one *have* occurred in real life: being told one Friday afternoon in my first year of teaching that my last period honors English class would be replaced by a section of Algebra 1 the next Monday comes to mind.

These harmless dreams are ones I would have off and on (as I suspect most of us do) depending on the time of year and associated level of anxiety. But here's a related dream I never did have—nor did anything close to it happen in real interactions with my students or their families. I realize now, though, that I should have been worrying more about this scenario, or the chronic underpreparation it represents, than about phantom exams or surprise teaching assignments. Permit me to narrate:

It's the evening of spring parent–teacher conferences. I sit down with a parent or guardian and pull from my carefully organized file folder the grade sheet for the student whose name falls next on the blue appointment card. On the grade report, perfect rows and columns announce the title of each assignment and the score the student earned on it, alongside the points possible. At the top of the sheet, the student's level of achievement in my class comes into neat focus, in a bolded percentage calculated to two decimal places of precision.

I've also written attendance information at the top of the page; parents like to know when their understanding of a student's attendance differs from the school's. The parent or guardian will also no doubt ask how the student can improve his or her grade, so I've taken the time to highlight some missing assignments. I've prepared all this information in advance to direct the conversation to its typically optimistic end, when the parent and I shake hands and thank each other for the time we've taken out of our busy schedules to talk with each other.

But this time the parent thanks me for all this information, perhaps just a little dismissively, and says, "I'm not all that interested in points and averages. I want to know how well my child is reading. What's he good at? What kinds of patterns are you noticing?" The classroom begins to spin. Unseen violins shriek wildly. But the parent persists: "And what are you doing to help him?"

If I had ever dreamed such a situation, I can imagine myself responding in a couple of different ways. In one, I bolt up and out of bed in a cold sweat, find my copy of *Mosaic of Thought* (Keene & Zimmerman, 1997), and vow again to transform some of its ideas into classroom practice. The parent has every right to ask such a question, and I need to figure out a way to get him or her an answer—quickly.

The other version of the response involves a shift into lucid dreaming. Just as I sometimes take control of dreams in which I'm flying (because I know it is so unreal that it has to be a concoction of my imagination), I realize that a parent asking focused, meaningful questions about my assessment of a high school student's reading ability is just *not* that likely to happen. In this version, I capitalize on the opportunity by starting to ask the kinds of questions that teachers often have of parents, but are too polite to ask. . . .

Unpacking My History with Assessment

I know it may seem odd to begin a book about reading assessment with a series of dreams, including a fictional one at that. But the topics of teaching and learning, preparation, expectations, anxiety, surprise, and uncertainty are actually quite germane to assessment, particularly school-based assessment. At the risk of indulging in too much analysis of my own dreams, let me take a moment to clarify what the ones I've shared do and don't have in common. The first is merely an anxious brain misfire, a representation of the fear of being helpless in a situation in which I actually had quite a bit of control. The second is more understandable. After all, it's impossible to be fully prepared for the situations that can and do come our way as teachers. In the hours between falling asleep grading and getting up for school the next day, sometimes our brains avenge themselves by playing tricks on us.

The third dream is more complicated. At the time I represent in that fictional dream, I had nearly complete control over what was taught and assessed in my classroom. But without a strong written curriculum, and with a relatively thin knowledge base about how adolescents read and develop as readers, I made a number of decisions about what to privilege and what to marginalize through assessment that I now see as inappropriate. The fact that a parent or guardian of one of the students in my class—a vested partner in the process of education—could ask a question so deeply related to one of the fundamental components of success in my class, and that I was completely unprepared to answer? That's truly frightening.

What I ended up assessing in my English classes (and hence best understanding about my students) was related to the traditional *stuff* of a language arts curriculum—response to literature, writing, grammar, vocabulary, and so forth—but it was also about compliance and completion of assignments. As I look back now, many of those assignments probably weren't all that important, and they definitely didn't give the students or me much information about how they were developing as readers. In essence, I was assessing student *engagement* with content in English, but I was unable to assess student engagement and growth in the key process of reading. To put it another way, I was meeting only one of the "dual goals" that Afflerbach (2004) challenges us to pursue—both "of understanding how students are learning content, *and* how their reading achievement is related to this learning" (p. 384, emphasis added).

I certainly wasn't alone in my department, school, or district in exhibiting a significant gap between *valuing* reading, a skill that is central to success in English (and in nearly

> Look at a student grade printout or the paper or online gradebook you keep. What do you seem to value based on the assessments recorded there? What information does your gradebook offer about students' content acquisition and development as readers? How closely do your core values as a teacher match the assessment information implied in grading documents that you share with students, families, other teachers, and administrators?

every other academic learning context), and actually being able to evaluate *growth* in reading. At a certain point, teachers in my school did realize that we needed some way to determine student grade-level equivalency and to look for evidence of growth over the course of a year. To that end, we began administering the Gates-MacGinitie reading assessment to our ninth and tenth graders. The test confirmed our suspicions: in classroom after classroom, our students were reading at vastly different levels, and many were significantly below grade level, even in honors classes. We gave the assessment again in the spring, but in between and afterward, we did not use the information we had gleaned to adjust what we taught or how we taught it.

These gaps—both between what we valued and what we assessed and between what we assessed and how we used the assessment information—left the English departments of the two high schools in my district vulnerable to a hostile takeover by a standardized assessment–crazed group of administrators who were hired specifically to close an achievement gap under a federal consent decree through the Office of Civil Rights. Without taking time to assess the state of our written English curriculum (which was weak) or our teachers' understanding of the relationships between curriculum, assessment, and instruction (which were not well developed), this administration demanded that we produce reading tests to be administered to our students every six to nine weeks.

We voiced concerns about the process, and these concerns were interpreted as resistance. We voiced a lack of knowledge about test construction, and our claims were ignored as passive noncompliance. Teams of us were pulled from class or paid outside of the school day to write reading assessments. A full-time job was created to copy all of these tests, coordinate their deployment, and oversee the distribution of reams of paper covered in red, yellow, and green ink, signifying a student's supposed level of mastery of any number of state standards. All of this went on despite our very open declaration of uncertainty about what the tests were actually assessing. We remained largely silent about our inability to respond to what the test results said (for fear of being called out on a gap in our professional knowledge), but that was certainly a significant issue as well.

I'd like to say that for the vast majority of us, these assessments did absolutely nothing to change our daily classroom lives. In truth, though, our students lost too many days of instruction to the administration of these tests. At one point, a colleague totaled the number of days devoted to this kind of assessment in her junior English class—including time spent taking practice ACTs, then the main component of our state test, and the state exam itself—and came up with fifteen. That's *three entire school weeks* of instruction lost to the administration of tests that teachers did not (and later, we learned, actually *could not*) translate into instructional change.

The other less obvious but just as damaging change this testing regime brought to our classrooms was the vilification of the word *assessment* and the adoption of a philosophical division between the acts of teaching and assessing. Let me be clear: at the worst moments of our district's testing craze, teachers were right to say, "Stop these assessments and let me teach!" But the fact that this desperate request applies to an unproductive assessment climate doesn't justify its overapplication to all kinds of assessment. For all the nightmares that testing created in our schools for a few years, principled classroom-based, inquiry-driven reading assessment is the only answer to the anxious dream I detailed at the start of this chapter. This book seeks to offer portraits of classroom practice that illustrate such assessment.

Assessment Rehab

Another of my goals for writing this book is to reclaim the word *assessment* for high school teachers who are rightfully charged with improving the reading ability of all their students. Since I've shared a bit about the unprincipled assessment activity I have been involved in, I'll also be transparent about the rehabilitation process I went through (or, more accurately, am going through) to repair my relationship with assessment. The components of my rehabilitation include the following:

> **Becoming very familiar with *Understanding by Design* (Wiggins & McTighe, 2005)**
> As I'll discuss later, goal clarity as represented through deep teacher knowledge and strong written curricula is an absolute necessity for effective assessment of reading (or of anything else, for that matter). Though I'm far from expert enough to recommend one theory of curriculum development over another, I do recommend that teachers read *Understanding by Design*, particularly the chapters on understanding and assessment. Since a significant goal of reading is understanding—and reading is a key process that facilitates understanding—you can in some ways treat the entire book as a text about reading. The authors' commonsense approach to the centrality of assessment in the teaching and learning process is incredibly valuable. Also useful for me is their reassurance that some things (such as how well an adolescent reads) are difficult to know; we need multiple, flexible measures to inform even our most tenuous sense of what most learners can do with text.

> **Participating in school-based professional learning communities (PLCs)**
> With their strong focus on collaborative curriculum development and checking for understanding and growth, professional learning communities (or, more aptly, the time invested in allowing such collaboration to flourish) have had a significant impact on my practice. As our school un-

derwent state-mandated restructuring, we committed to setting aside at least one hour a week for each course (most core curriculum courses for ninth and tenth graders meet four hours a week) to determine what we value instructionally and to examine student work that helps us check on progress toward our goals. I cannot agree more with the assertion in the International Reading Association (IRA)–National Council of Teachers of English (NCTE) *Standards for the Assessment of Reading and Writing*, Revised Edition (the 2010 document by the Joint Task Force on Assessment of IRA and NCTE that is the basis of this book; more on those standards in a moment) that "improving teachers' assessment expertise requires ongoing professional development, coaching, and access to professional learning communities . . . [because] teachers need to feel safe to share, discuss, and critique their own work in public forums with their peers" (p. 14). Central to my improved view of the role of assessment was our determination to keep the process of examining students' progress against our stated goals rooted in authentic classroom work and fueled by teacher-led conversations about that work.*

Reading a range of very smart books on formative assessment

Books such as *Transformative Assessment* (Popham, 2008) and *Checking for Understanding* (Fisher & Frey, 2007) offer both strong theory and practical application of assessment as an integral part of the instructional cycle. Still, although they convinced me that purposeful short-cycle assessment was worth investigating, almost uniformly the books focus on measuring understanding of content, not the actual process of reading (recall Afflerbach's comment about the need to look for evidence of both). They occasionally offer examples from English classrooms, but these examples typically showcase the development and assessment of student writing, where the product is more visible. I found myself continuing to wonder what formative assessment in reading would look like for adolescents.

Picking up a copy of the revised IRA–NCTE *Standards for the Assessment of Reading and Writing* (2010)

When I was at the International Reading Association convention in 2010, I grabbed the *Standards* as an impulse purchase in the bookstore checkout line. Its compact nature made it easy to start and stop reading between sessions. These assessment standards, the undergirding document of this book, gave clarity of language and solidity of philosophy to my growing understanding of how I could help my students read better by getting smarter at learning what they could do. (Note: The *Standards*, minus the cases studies and glossary, are reprinted in the front matter of this book. The *Standards* in their entirety are also available as a free download from both the IRA and NCTE websites.)

---

*For more information about the values of and structures that support such work, see the NCTE 2011 Policy Research Brief on communities of practice at www.ncte.org/library/NCTEFiles/Resources/Journals/CC/0212nov2011/CC0212Policy.pdf.

The IRA–NCTE assessment standards (hereafter referred to as the SARW) address assessment in many forms (see Figure 1.1), but this book focuses primarily on what Shepard (2000) calls *classroom assessment*, a kind of assessment different from assessment for grades or for external accountability purposes. The purpose of this kind of assessment is to "be used as a part of instruction to support and enhance learning," rather than as "an occasion to mete out rewards and punishments" (Shepard, p. 10). The SARW offer a similar view of "productive and powerful assessments," referring to them as "the formative assessments that occur in the daily activities of the classroom" (p. 13). I mention this distinction because the other kinds of assessment—summative assessments that generate grades and standardized tests that hold schools (and certain agents within the schools) accountable—will still be administered and do have a certain value within the system.

But the kind of classroom assessment you'll be reading about in this book—assessment that intends to be as consonant with the SARW as my colleagues and I are able to be at this point in our professional practice—happens in addition to and alongside those other kinds of assessment. Sometimes the three kinds of assessment—formative, summative, and standardized—will overlap, but part of the story of professional growth this book documents is my district's eventual understanding that tests such as the ACT and tests modeled on it (such as our so-called quarterly

---

Figure 1.1: Understanding formative and summative assessment.

The SARW offer these comparative definitions of *formative* and *summative* assessment. Although these definitions, quoted directly, discuss the typical form these assessments might take (e.g., a portfolio conference versus an end-of-chapter test), I view the most significant difference between the two kinds of assessment as *whether the teacher is able to change instruction as a result of what is learned through it*. In other words, an assessment given to two students could be formative for one student and summative for the other if the teacher learns something new about one student and not the other, leading to a change in instruction for one and not the other. An assessment can be labeled as formative or summative only *after* it is given and the student and teacher have an opportunity to act on the information (or not).

Formative assessment	*Summative assessment*
Formative assessment, often referred to as assessment *for* learning, is the assessment that is done before and during teaching to inform instruction. It is assessment that informs instruction. Formative assessment includes things like teacher–student conferences, listening in on student book discussions, taking records of children's oral reading, examining students' writing pieces, and so forth. Though these assessments might be standardized, they often are not. To be formative, an assessment must affect instruction. (SARW, p. 49)	Summative assessment, often referred to as assessment *of* learning, is the after-the-fact assessment in which we look back at what students have learned, such as end-of-course or end-of-year examinations. The most familiar forms are the end-of-year standardized tests, though in classrooms we also assess students' learning at the end of a unit. These assessments are likely to be uniform or standardized. (SARW, p. 52)

Reflect on the kinds of conversations around reading assessment that typically occur at your school. Are high-stakes standardized assessments the only ones that get any legitimate "air time" at meetings and staff development sessions? What happens when teachers challenge the implied authority of state reading test scores?

reading assessments)—*do not and cannot ever* give us the fine-grained, context-specific information we need in order to teach our kids more effectively, no matter how much we want those tests to do so, and in spite of what their designers might tell us. The SARW call for stakeholders within a school community to avoid "endow[ing] test scores with the power to tell more than they are able" (p. 18). It's easy to tell administrators that most standardized tests "do not adequately reflect a complex model of literacy" (p. 18), but it's significantly more challenging to offer an alternative view.

I've found that demonstrating achievement gains resulting from purposeful, careful, effective classroom assessment is the only antidote to such test worship, and I count this as another goal of this book.

Toward a More Principled Role as Assessor

A key image in my third teacher nightmare (the one that I realize now is actually scarier for never having happened in real life) is the student grade printout, which is nominally full of classroom assessments (to misuse Shepard's term). In reality, this printout is rivaled only by the Scantron sheet as the document that symbolizes the flaws in our current era of school assessment. The official, computer-generated appearance of these grade sheets hides the hundreds of human choices involved in assessment—not only in the myriad scores awarded to all the various tasks, but also which and what kinds of tasks get counted in the first place. Because the mathematics of the grade is made to seem unquestionable, the much more important concerns—namely, the principles determining what should be assessed, and how—are given a free pass as well.

Sometimes in our desire to be efficient, accurate, and authoritative, we overlook that which is most central to our work as teachers. The SARW remind us that assessment, particularly in a culture that puts so much emphasis on corporate standardized tests, is too often represented as "merely a technical process." We have to challenge ourselves to remember that assessment is, in fact, "always representational and interpretive because it involves representing children's development" (p. 9). I find it important to acknowledge that central tension within our profession, particularly in regard to adolescent literacy development, given the overwhelming misconception that high school students are "done" learning how to read by the time they are teens.

I was very intentional with the title for the first chapter of this book. I wanted to be clear that I would be airing a bit of individual and institutional laundry here;

it's impossible for me to write about assessment without detailing some of the missteps I've taken or been involved in. In choosing the word *unprincipled* to describe my identity as a reading assessor, however, I hoped to suggest that while I was definitely doing some things wrong, I was also stumbling into doing some things right as well. I simply didn't have a clear and unwavering mission for assessment. In the language of the SARW, I was not "aware of and deliberate about" my role as an assessor, so I couldn't judge whether my assessments were effective (p. 13). Getting students to comply with my requests for work in order to generate points to put on the grade sheet is the most unifying reason I can see in my early classroom practice, but that one is almost too base to admit (though, of course, it's largely true).

When I think back to the changing tasks that showed up on my students' grade sheets over the first few years of my career, I do see that I was a conscious experimenter with how I assessed as I developed as a beginning teacher. As pressure over lagging reading scores mounted in our school and beyond, I rather clumsily pursued a number of investigations into what my students could do as readers. Most basically, I started to ask students to *read* on the tests I gave at the end of a unit or major work. Borrowing perhaps too liberally from the tactics of the professors of my undergraduate literature surveys, I would ask students to read excerpts from the book under study and write short critical responses. Definitely borrowing too liberally from the ACT or the Advanced Placement exam, I would pull short excerpts from the novel or play we'd read and ask a series of multiple-choice questions getting at comprehension and application of pertinent literary elements.

But these assessments did little for me as a teacher and even less, I suspect, for my students. I might have pondered surprises or felt pleased with some good results, but once the numbers landed on the grade sheet, the assessment's function in the instructional process was over. Using the formal language of assessment, these tests were completely summative because they offered me almost no information that would help me change instruction, as a formative assessment must.

So even these, my best attempts to assess reading, were thwarted by a series of "lacks" that, taken together, get at the heart of the value of the SARW:

1. I didn't quite know what I was assessing.
2. I didn't have a good enough, clear enough—principled enough—reason for assessing whatever it was I was assessing.
3. Had I known what I really wanted to assess, I still wouldn't have known how to assess it.
4. I didn't have the curricular or instructional means to respond effectively to any information I gathered through the assessments I *did* deliver.

We all enter the classroom with certain pre-conceived stances toward reading assessment. For many of us, that stance involves some variation of "That's not my job!" Take some time to reflect on what assessment attitudes and practices you brought with you as a result of schooling and your own past experiences. What new habits and practices have you developed over the course of your career? What new skills and insights might you be interested in developing?

The rest of this chapter and, indeed, much of this book continues to trace my journey of "assessment rehab" as I learned, and continue to learn, how to get into the heads of my students as readers and thinkers in order to find out, as best I can, what I need to do next to teach them effectively.

Happily, I've not been alone during this process of growth. As an instructional coach at a large comprehensive high school and codirector of a National Writing Project site, I have the privilege of working side by side with smart, dedicated teachers nearly year-round. For this particular project, eight teachers at Central High School allowed me to collaborate with them through my role as a coach as teaching and learning occurred in their classrooms:

Will Aldridge, Social Studies—Will is a third-year teacher at Central. Currently he splits his time between social science (where you'll read about him teaching ninth-grade Ancient Civilizations) and a support class called AVID (Advancement via Individual Determination).

Chris Belt, English—In his second year of teaching, Chris teaches honors and regular-level ninth graders. The class you'll see him working with is a first-hour honors English class preparing for and reading *To Kill a Mockingbird*. Chris is a teacher consultant with the University of Illinois Writing Project.

Kathy Decker, English—Kathy has been teaching for eight years, all at Central High School. She teaches accelerated and academic-level juniors. The class you'll read about was reading Frederick Douglass's autobiography and *A Lesson Before Dying*; the students have diverse backgrounds that cross the spectrum of ability and motivational levels. Kathy is a teacher consultant with the Eastern Illinois University Writing Project.

Liz Dietz, English—Liz is a first-year educator who teaches sophomore and senior English. You'll see some of the work she and her honors-level sophomore students did while reading George Orwell's *Animal Farm*.

Nikelle Miller, Science—Nikki has taught a range of science courses over sixteen years in a variety of settings. Before coming to Central, where she teaches biology and accelerated biology, she was named Chicagoland Lutheran Education Foundation High School Teacher of the Year (2005).

Stephanie Royse, Special Education/Reading—A second-year teacher, Stephanie teaches self-contained reading classes for students receiving special education services and co-teaches with sophomore English teachers.

Faith Sharp, Science—Now in her fourth year of her second career as a high school teacher (she previously conducted research in microbiology), Faith teaches biology and accelerated biology. She is actively involved with Project NEURON at the University of Illinois and coaches the academic teams for Science Olympiad and Worldwide Youth in Science and Engineering (WYSE).

Gary Slotnick, English—Gary is the English department chair and teaches Advanced Placement English, honors sophomores, and regular-level senior literature. He has taught for eighteen years—eight at middle school, ten at high school. You'll read about his work with a co-taught senior English class during a short story unit and while reading *Hamlet*.

As you might assume from the list of teachers participating in this project, most of the classroom scenarios you'll be reading about depict students who are reading as part of the day-to-day processes of developing understanding of content in their subject area courses. On the other hand, the scenarios from Stephanie Royse's class and my own come from high school reading classes, where students have been placed for additional support. Knowing that the work that goes on in our classes differs from other, more content-focused courses, I have worked to make the assessment and response techniques as applicable to other situations as possible.

As you continue to read, you may be surprised that in a book about reading *assessment* what you're actually seeing are descriptions of *teaching*. Sure, I offer some tools and techniques we developed to gather information about what students could and couldn't do with text in a particular situation. But the SARW hold that the "central function of assessment . . . is . . . to improve the quality of teaching and learning and thereby to increase the likelihood that all members of the society will acquire a full and critical literacy" (p. 16). Therefore, just as important as the tools and "results" of assessment—in fact, more important if we're to reclaim assessment's centrality to the acts of teaching and learning—is the interconnection between teaching goals, assessment, and response through instruction.

Goal Clarity: The Key to Assessment

Confusing, ineffective, or harmful assessment can have many root causes, but none is as likely as the lack of goal clarity. One way to think about assessment is as the *search for evidence of a change that you've worked to develop*. If you don't have a really clear picture of what that change is, seeking evidence of it is bound to be frustrating at best and damaging at its worst. The popular literature about educational assessment makes this case well, and it's a good point, but the resulting proliferation of standards (and eventual development of sub-standards, benchmarks, and performance indicators) is being sold too simplistically as the remedy. Some otherwise useful professional literature on assessment falls into the unfortunate habit of suggesting that teachers need to divide and subdivide challenging content and complex processes—such as those involved with reading—into the most minute, observable pieces, often referred to as "learning targets." When assessing reading development in adolescents, however, I feel it is crucial not to confuse goal *simplicity* with goal *clarity*. Reading may have components that are conceptually separable, but in reality they are not separate; assessment of the parts does not necessarily give us a realistic picture of the whole.

When I think back to my school's earliest efforts to make reading assessment and instruction a cross-disciplinary endeavor, I recall using the framework offered by our state's test, then the ACT. The literature about the ACT divided reading into eight skills: determining meanings of words, finding the main idea, making generalizations, and so forth. Desperate for a framework on which to hang our professional development efforts as well as our own nascent understandings of reading, we used those skills as our operational definition of reading—without giving much regard to crucial issues such as text complexity, current level of performance, prior knowledge, and the cognitive and metacognitive processes that fuel the act of reading. We fell into the trap that the SARW warn against—"fragment[ing] literacy rather than represent[ing] its complexity . . . [and] omit[ting] important aspects of literacy such as self-initiated learning, questioning author's bias, perspective taking, multiple literacies, social interactions around literacy, metacognitive strategies, and literacy dispositions" (p. 17).

While there are many places a teacher can go to begin or continue to build a strong knowledge base about reading (see the annotated bibliography at the end of this book for some titles I've found particularly useful), I'm going to rely here on a framework set forth in Stephen Kucer's chapter "What We Know about the Nature of Reading," a framework built out of Kucer's research (Kucer, 2008; see also Kucer, 1991; Kucer, 2005; Kucer & Silva, 2006) and the work of NCTE's Commission on Reading. I like this framework because, above all, it rings true with my own experiences as a reader, as a developing teacher of reading, and as a parent who has had the delight of observing and supporting a son as he learns to read. In addition to those reasons, Kucer's framework offers a certain clarity about reading that has helped me situate my assessment practice. But it also possesses a richness that constantly challenges me not to oversimplify the act of reading in ways that most standardized assessment and popular packaged curricula tend to do.

Before summarizing some of the key information from Kucer's conception of reading, I should mention that it is possible to employ and respond to classroom-based reading assessments such as the ones described in the chapters that follow without an exceptionally strong background in understanding how people read. While I certainly concur with the SARW's assertion that the "more knowledgeable teachers are on the subjects of reading and writing and the more observant they are of students' literate behavior, the more productive their assessments will be"

(p. 14), teachers who feel undereducated about reading can rest assured that the assessment processes I highlight will actually prompt and facilitate a certain degree of this learning for them when they assess their students. We don't have the luxury of waiting until we all feel *expert* in reading to start inquiring into how our students are developing as readers and thinkers; rather, such assessment-based inquiry is a natural and effective way to begin developing that expertise.

Kucer's framework (2008) suggests that reading possesses four *dimensions*: linguistic, cognitive, sociocultural, and developmental. The use of the word *dimensions*, as opposed to, say, *components* or *stages*, is appealing. Imagine moving a large piece of furniture from one room in your house to another. The most important dimension of a couch, for instance, might seem to be its length because you need to make sure it will fit along the wall in the room to which you're moving it. But when you get to a doorway, the length of the couch suddenly doesn't matter as much as its width. If the couch is too wide for the doorway, the concern might then become the height of the couch as you turn it on its side for a better fit.

In Kucer's framework, the word *dimensions* similarly suggests that linguistic, cognitive, sociocultural, and developmental factors (not even *factors* is a good substitute) are always and inseparably present in an act of reading. One may be more salient in a given situation, and we may be looking at only one in a particular assessment setting, but that doesn't mean the other three aren't operating. We're simply choosing to ignore them for the moment because, after all, we cannot attend to everything all the time. It's important, though, to keep reminding ourselves that even when we privilege one dimension (and this book will indeed privilege some dimensions over others), the others don't "go away." Making a commitment to supporting our adolescent readers in all four dimensions gives us the best chance of success.

Kucer explains that in the *linguistic dimension*, the reader is "code breaker," and must call upon all of his or her resources relating to the systemic relationships between written language, sound, and sense. This dimension, like all of the dimensions, is complex, but thankfully for teachers of most older adolescents, the requisite fundamental understandings of letter-sound relationships, grammar, and syntax are so deeply ingrained as to be invisible. Most readers in high school have achieved a high degree of automaticity in this dimension, and they don't have to spend much cognitive energy here. This is not to say that cognitive energy isn't *required* in this dimension: older students who struggle with fluency give us clear evidence that these dimensions are not magically tied to age or grade level. Ignoring a dimension simply because we believe a student should already be "beyond it" is faulty thinking. Just as faulty, however, is the belief that focusing *only* on a particular dimension will lead to improvement in the realm of literacy development as a whole, as some programmatic assessment and intervention approaches suggest.

Kucer's second dimension, the *cognitive dimension*, depicts the reader as meaning-maker and is, I suspect, the dimension that will be most familiar to secondary teachers. After all, we think of younger students as focusing heavily on the linguistic dimension because they are "learning to read." Once that's out of the way, students are asked to "read to learn" and make meaning from text that supports learning in the various content areas. "A cognitive discussion of literacy," Kucer explains, "concerns those mental processes, strategies, or procedures that the individual engages so as to construct meaning" (2008, p. 35). We know quite a bit about those processes and strategies now (predicting, visualizing, connecting, and the like), and we understand that they need to be modeled and taught as well—to the extent that they have in some cases become the overt focus of instruction to the detriment of the complexity of understanding (Fisher & Frey, 2008b).

Factors such as the reader's background and experience with language, as well as his or her purpose(s) for reading, create a frame for a reading event in which the reader uses the aforementioned strategies and processes as he or she "construct[s] an understanding of the text . . . [and] monitors and evaluates the meanings being generated" (Kucer, 2008, p. 37). Adding to the complexity (and intriguing beauty) of this dimension: *as a result of the exertion of all this cognition, the reader is cognitively changed.* When, for example, a student summons background knowledge about race and racism to comprehend and respond to a chapter from *To Kill a Mockingbird*, that student's background knowledge and understanding of race and racism are themselves challenged and expanded by the interaction between text and reader. What teachers look for through assessment, then, is a combination of the cognitive processes that lead to change (which are, by definition, invisible) and evidence of the change itself (which is also invisible). These two concepts—on their own and together—become a major focus of the assessment work portrayed in this book.

The *sociocultural* dimension of reading, representing "the reader's knowledge of how to use texts in socially appropriate ways and the ability to read critically" (Kucer, 2008, p. 43), is one that likely will seem least familiar to most teachers, but not because it is the least important. When teachers are given a moment to think about what they themselves value most about reading and its uses—from personal enrichment to political engagement and everywhere between and beyond—it's often the dimension we care most about. However, schools have historically attempted to strip literacy of this dimension, largely to make it easier to teach and assess. Traditional literature anthologies, with their prepackaged focus on skills and strategies accessed through a prescribed reading list that has been selected and sequenced with no regard for the diversity of learners in the room, are the most obvious way in which school-based reading is denied its sociocultural dimension. Personal agency and social contexts interact with literacy development in significant ways, and school-based approaches to reading and learning ignore that reality at their peril. Students' refusal to engage in the learning process is the costly result of such a denial of the sociocultural dimension of reading.

Broadly construed and consonant with the IRA–NCTE standards, assessment itself should never become the *goal* of reading, as I suspect it sometimes seems to students. I imagine all of us harbor a fear that students leave high school believing that the purpose of reading was to answer someone else's questions about texts they didn't care about. We want to teach and assess reading in a way that defies narrow definitions of the complexity of reading and facilitates the nourishment of the generally underserved sociocultural dimension of reading.

Kucer's last dimension of reading, the *developmental* dimension, posits reading as an act of inquiry and frames readers as scientists who use the other dimensions collectively to achieve desired outcomes as they "encounter reading experiences that involve using reading in new and novel ways" (2008, p. 50). This dimension challenges the dominant school-based assessment paradigm of assessing for *mastery* and asks us instead to support a "learner's growth in the ability to effectively and efficiently apply . . . literacy strategies across an ever-widening range of situations" (p. 52). As part of this dimension, Kucer asks us to think of students as *constantly becoming literate*, rather than *being (or not being) literate*. Doing so asks us to rethink assessment not as something that happens, but rather as something that is always happening, an idea I take up next.

Reading Assessment as Purposeful Inquiry

Recall my comments about the Scantron and printed grade sheets—the twin relics of flawed assessment. Among the many problems I have with these documents is that they tend to suck the life out what should be a vibrant and active process: the act and art of figuring out what our students can do and seeking information that will help us better instruct them along the way to doing even more. I've already mentioned some authors whose work is helpful for developing a sense of this kind of teaching stance—James Popham, Doug Fisher and Nancy Frey, and Lorrie Shepard are certainly great places to start—but no single line of thinking has been more influential for me than Frank Serafini's 2000–2001 article from *The Reading Teacher* titled "Three Paradigms of Assessment: Measurement, Procedure, and Inquiry." In it, he builds off the work of Short and Burke (1994) to explain that if our concept of effective curriculum has shifted from rote memorization of facts to more active, constructivist inquiry (as we now understand reading to be), our sense of assessment has to shift along with it from discrete acts of measurement to "a process of inquiry, and a process of interpretation, used to promote reflection concerning students' understandings, attitudes, and literate abilities" (Serafini, 2000–2001, p. 387). Though I know there are those who believe that the primary purpose of content area reading for adolescents is "hunting for facts," a more informed and humane understanding frames reading as a constructive act in which students make meaning by combining their lived experiences with the content on the page. Such a view demands that we strive for the kind of assessment that Serafini describes as inquiry.

In addition to the extremes of assessment as either measurement or inquiry, Serafini offers an intermediate paradigm of assessment as *process*, in which the teacher is focused primarily on "assessment procedures, not [on] the underlying purposes of the assessment program, or the epistemological stance" (2000–2001, p. 386). This paradigm aptly describes my previously recounted efforts as a novice English teacher: I was curious to know more about my students as readers, and I engaged in some thoughtful processes to start inquiring. But since the grade sheet was, in fact, the ultimate purpose of any assessment I engaged in, I was stuck in that middle ground and found myself unable to use information to make changes in my teaching or in my students' development as readers. Without a clear inquiry framework, I was unable to answer the SARW's emphatic call to become the most important agent of assessment in my classroom, constantly asking questions with the goal of "construct[ing] an understanding of [my] students as literate individuals" (p. 13).

The portraits of classroom practice in the pages that follow document teachers and students who are determined to make the challenging paradigmatic shift to assessment as inquiry. Within any classroom, the accumulated historical attitudes toward and beliefs about assessment, oftentimes framing assessment as an isolated event rather than an ongoing process, are significant and can create barriers to new approaches. Not only do teachers' beliefs about assessment matter, but departmental and district policy statements and the tools we use to facilitate assessment also figure prominently. And all this says nothing of the significance of the attitudes toward and histories with assessment that students bring with them.

The SARW explain that the inquiry questions that guide effective assessment are "rarely well formulated or structured at the outset. Rather, structure emerges through the process" (p. 49) of asking questions, examining work, collaborating with peers, and asking new questions. The potential scope of such inquiry can be daunting. After all, if secondary teachers were responsible for fewer students, we likely wouldn't be so drawn to efficiency-oriented tools such as electronic grade books and Scantron sheets in the first place. Within the context of that struggle, however, you'll see the teachers I focus on in this book making positive changes in classroom practice in direct response to information gained from assessment, as well as gaining voice to communicate more persuasively with administrators about issues of curriculum and assessment. Most important, you'll see evidence of improved student reading and content acquisition as a result of adults who are working smarter (and sometimes harder) to support them through principled reading assessment.

Chapter 2 continues to expand on a definition of inquiry-based reading assessment, offering a number of tools developed from two high school reading classes that embody the questions two teachers had about their students. The chapter also offers a theoretical and practical argument for authentic reading assessment, using the assessment terminology of *construct* and *consequential validity* to put standardized reading tests in their appropriate place. Chapter 3 broadens in focus from the assessment tools to the classroom routines that support response to information gained from assessment, illustrating the process of formative assessment. Chapter 4 shifts focus again, framing the inquiry of three classroom teachers not only to improve instruction but also to reflect critically on their own professional practice. Finally, moving from the classroom to other contexts for assessment inquiry, Chapter 5 offers a vision for assessment as an act of caring for our students, a vision that then needs to include as many stakeholders as possible in the processes of teaching, learning, and assessing.

Chapter Two

Seeking Truth, Considering Consequences: Getting into Students' Heads through Inquiry–Based Assessment

Teachers and schools assess students' ability to read for a range of reasons: to seek evidence of progress toward certain goals, to guide and improve instruction, to sort and rank students, to report to various stakeholders, and more. As I mentioned in the opening chapter, the kinds of assessment you'll read about in this book tend to focus on those purposes more toward the beginning of this list than the end. But, as I've come to understand in so many aspects of education, what at first appears to be a set of distinct purposes quickly blurs into a mosaic of overlapping intentions. Effective teaching requires us, for example, to assess learners in order to sort students into flexible groups as a means of improving instruction. Additionally, when we consider that the student is the most significant stakeholder in an act of assessment, as the IRA–NCTE *Standards for the Assessment of Reading and Writing* (SARW) suggest, the function of classroom feedback takes on central importance. Providing assessment-based feedback to a broad range of stakeholders also becomes a means of maintaining teacher autonomy when ineffective practice is mandated through distant administrative decisions, an issue I'll take up in both this chapter and the closing chapter of the book.

We can agree, then, that teachers may have a variety of well-intentioned purposes for assessment and that purposes can overlap in complex ways, but the SARW are emphatic in the assertion that "the *consequences* of an assessment procedure are the first and most important consideration in establishing the validity of the assessment" (p. 22, emphasis added). I was at first struck by this statement for its incongruity with what I had been taught to think about the word *validity* in relation to assessment. *Construct validity*, the aspect of validity most of us learned about as part of our teacher training, refers to the extent to which an assessment measures what it purports to measure. Fulfilling this aspect when assessing adolescent readers is, of course, challenging enough; I'll give it more attention throughout this chapter. But the SARW's notion of validity tied to consequences raises the stakes for the integrity of assessment to the level of instructional response.

Afflerbach (2011) reports that this second notion of validity, *consequential validity*, grew out of the awareness of the consequences—rewards and sanctions—related to high-stakes standardized testing in the late 1980s. Despite the term's origin in the wake of large-scale testing, it is just as applicable to the assessment practices in all of our classrooms. What happens to the student as a result of taking a test (including accounting for the instructional time devoted to participating in the assessment) is as central to the test's educational validity as the quality of its construction. In this chapter, I share portraits of assessment that illustrate the challenges and successes associated with striving for validity in both senses, construct and consequential. What seem to be separate concepts, two *kinds* of validity, are intimately related. When an assessment, for example, asks students to do more of what we think of as "real reading" (i.e., doing more than answering multiple-choice questions about contextless passages), we have a much better chance of being able to use the information it gives us to shape instruction. In Figure 2.1, I summarize the ways in which I differentiate construct validity from consequential validity and how an inquiry approach to assessment connects the two.

> Think about an assessment you've administered that allowed you to improve instruction, either in the moment or at a later time. What was it about that assessment that allowed you to do so? How was that assessment different from one that might have been more of a "point-generating" event?

Moving beyond the Limits of Standardized Truth and Consequences

To help illustrate the relationships between construct validity, consequential validity, and the rewarding challenges of taking an inquiry-based approach to assessment, I'll share some experiences from my colleague Stephanie Royse, who teaches a year-

Figure 2.1: How do construct validity, consequential validity, and an inquiry stance toward assessment support one another?

Determining Construct Validity	**Determining Consequential Validity**
Given our best understanding of what the act of reading is, does the assessment we use offer insight into how the student "measures up" against that understanding? In other words, have we created an assessment that accounts for the act of reading in its complicated fullness? • Are we allowed to observe both process and product? • Are we privileging precision (e.g., the student can answer exactly 6 out of 10 questions) over accuracy and richness of information? • If so, what do we lose or gain in the process?	Are we using assessments in a way that helps us create appropriate and ethical pedagogy for the students in our classes? • Are we making both immediate and long-term adjustments to what and how we teach that student? • Is the student in any way *harmed* by the assessment? • Given a range of assessments in a course, are we able to build a fairly good mental model of our students as readers and thinkers?

Validity and an Inquiry Approach to Reading Assessment

A concern for construct and consequential validity undergirds an inquiry-based approach to assessment. As teachers, we should constantly be inquiring into our own practices as readers. How do we make sense of text? How do our stores of (and gaps in) background knowledge allow and impede our ability to interpret and understand what we read? These questions help us build assessments with strong construct validity.

A central question for inquiry that has both construct and consequential validity then becomes: *How are my students making sense of the text they read in my class?*

• Perhaps starting with the preceding question, develop a question (or set of questions) you need the answer to in order to continue instruction.
• Select text that's right for the question(s), right for the group, and core to the disciplinary work you'd be doing anyway.
• Use the full range of possible classroom structures (whole-class think-alouds for teaching and reteaching, small-group work, or individual feedback/conferences) to respond to what you learn through the assessment.
• Don't expect miracles—older learners don't necessarily develop at the same rates as younger ones—but do expect and look carefully for signs of growth.

long reading course for students receiving special education services. When you walk into Stephanie's reading class, a makeshift classroom with temporary dividers for walls, you'll see posted co-constructed charts that identify and remind students of some powerful reading strategies effective readers use as they process and respond to text. You'll hear Stephanie demonstrating fluent reading and modeling through think-alouds that show how she makes sense of text. Students take turns reading high-interest fiction that matches Stephanie's best sense of her students' current levels of assisted performance. Students ask and answer questions, both verbally and in writing, to build and verify their understanding of what they're reading and learning. In other words, this is a secondary reading class in which many things are going very, very well.

The students in Stephanie's class were assigned there in large part because of their low performance on standardized reading tests. Schools continue to rely on standardized tests to determine placement in reading support programs, despite these assessments' overwhelming tendency to oversimplify student "success" or "failure" and the paucity of insight they offer teachers into students' abilities to decode, identify unfamiliar words, read fluently, and construct meaning from text (Riddle Buly & Valencia, 2002; Dennis, 2008; Dennis 2009–2010; Rasinski et al., 2005; Rupp & Lesaux, 2006) (see Figure 2.2). Stephanie was interested in moving past the "standardized truth"—that her students were not reading as well as nearly all of their grade-level peers—and wanted to look for information about her students that could help them develop as readers. Knowing that the limited construct validity of the standardized assessments leads almost certainly to low consequential validity, she needed to inquire further into her students' abilities, habits, and dispositions as readers to know how to respond effectively to their needs.

When I visited Stephanie's class, students were learning about Greek mythology and the elements of story structure while reading Rick Riordan's *Percy Jackson and the Olympians: The Lightning Thief*. Because Stephanie was interested in gaining more insight into what her students were thinking as they read, she had them stop occasionally to write whatever they were thinking at the moment on a sticky note. Stephanie had been working with students to understand the connection between

---

Figure 2.2: The IRA–NCTE SARW on standardized reading tests.

The SARW offer teachers a number of ways to think about the limitations of reading tests that have grown to become the most politically influential forces in our profession. We know these kinds of assessments are not enough. The challenge for classroom teachers, then, involves moving beyond critique and into inquiry around ways in which our professional expertise can be extended and shaped to achieve the goals for assessment that standardized tests so often cannot.

- **From the section "The Nature of Language"**
  "Language does not contain meaning; rather, meaning is constructed in the social relationships within which language is used. . . .
       . . . Meaning may vary from one person to another. . . . Thus, individuals make different sense of apparently similar language to the extent that their cultural and personal histories do not coincide. Consequently, when we attempt to standardize a test (by making it the same for everyone), we make the tenuous assumption that students will all make the same meaning from the language of our instructions and the language of the individual items." (pp. 3–4)

- **From the section "The Assessment of Language"**
  "That texts can (and should) be read from different perspectives must be taken as a certainty—a goal of schooling not to be disrupted by assessment practices that pretend otherwise. To assert through a multiple-choice test that a piece of text has only one meaning is unacceptable, given what we know about language." (p. 7)

- **From Standard 1: The interests of the student are paramount in assessment.**
  "Traditionally, group-administered, machine-scorable tests have not encouraged students to reflect constructively on their reading and writing, have not provided specific and timely feedback, and generally have not provided high-quality information about students. Consequently, they have seemed unlikely to serve the best interests of students. However, this need not be the case if they are able to provide timely, high-quality information to students." (pp. 12–13)

- **From Standard 4: Assessment must reflect and allow for critical inquiry into curriculum and instruction.**
  "Even when [reading and writing] standards come closer to representing . . . features of complex literacy, high-stakes assessments rarely address the difficult-to-measure standards, opting instead to focus on content that is easier and more expedient to assess using inexpensive test formats." (p. 17)

reading and active thinking, so they had little trouble making the next step to formalizing their thoughts in writing.

This technique of asking students to write what they're thinking as they read is readily applicable in any classroom context, with any reading assignment (I share a version of this strategy from a biology class toward the end of the chapter). Chances are your students have been asked to annotate text or share their thoughts while they read before—the idea of using sticky notes for purposes such as these is far from revolutionary. What can be revolutionary, though, is the purposeful move from "sticky note as activity"—which can certainly be valuable in its own right to help students understand the central truth that reading is active thinking—to using these brief student responses as a first step toward inquiry-based assessment. This shift, by the way, is an example of the difference Serafini (2000–2001) theorizes between assessment as process and assessment as inquiry, as I discuss next.

The responses in Figure 2.3 come from Richard, a ninth grader. When Stephanie and I met to investigate together what Richard and his classmates were revealing about themselves as thinkers (see the left-hand column only), Stephanie could see right away that Richard was asking questions and making sense of the story. He was noticing characters' motivations ("She like him to be on her team for she can win because of his power"), commenting on developing plot lines ("Some of the kid can go home because they do not have power"), and detecting shifting relationships between characters ("His dad do not like Annabeth's mom," "Percy and Luke [are] become friends"). Richard's annotations were also telling Stephanie that he could do more than restate; some of his thoughts suggest a degree of inference and prediction that not all of her students were exhibiting. She was already gathering the evidence that told her Richard would benefit from instruction with more emphasis on inference and higher grade-level text for independent work than some of his peers could currently handle.

As Stephanie and I read the sticky notes, we were constantly saying things like "That's really interesting, but I want to know more" and "I wonder what the student did with that thought." Finding yourself with more questions than answers is indeed a hallmark of approaching assessment as an act of dynamic inquiry. Stephanie and I had previously discussed that, particularly for older students, we see a need to move beyond cognitive strategy work ("I'm making a connection") to metacognition and awareness of when their habits of thought are supporting comprehension ("This connection helps me understand because . . ."). Thus, our question shifted from "What can students do with this text?" to the much more complex question, "How aware are students of whether their thinking is supporting their understanding?" To pursue this question, Stephanie reread the section with her students and asked them to look back at their responses through a metacognitive lens. Stephanie prompted the students to tell her *why* they thought what they thought and to assess whether the thought was useful in helping them comprehend, or if they were just writing something down to complete the task. If students had asked a question, she suggested they think about whether their question was answered through their reading or whether they needed to reread or read more to find out the answer.

Look again at Richard's responses (Figure 2.3), this time noting his extended thinking in the right-hand column. This is very likely the first time Richard was asked to think about his thoughts about reading in this way, so it is no surprise that we had difficulty drawing easy conclusions from his responses. In some cases, Richard was able to explain a bit more about the conclusions he came to or the evidence he used; other times the connection between initial and extended response is less clear or merely a repetition. Stephanie did notice that Richard was able to respond most strategically to the question he had asked ("Why is Luke being nice to Percy . . . [?]"), noting that he needed to "Read more." When the class continued reading, Richard went back to his note and explained that he thought Luke was being nice because Percy didn't know anyone else at the camp.

Figure 2.3: Richard's initial thoughts (sticky notes arranged from top to bottom on the left) and further thinking (on the right; each note refers to one of the numbered thoughts from the left, though not in physical proximity).

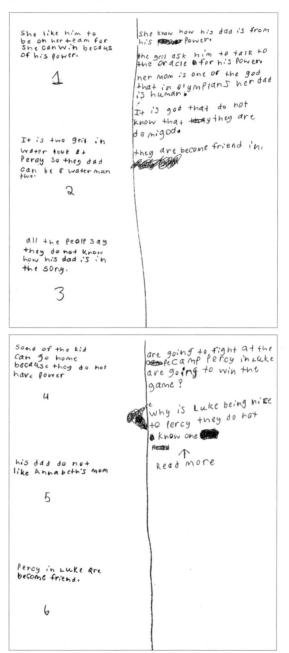

Stephanie's inquiry began with the deceptively simple question, "What are my kids thinking as they read?" She then became interested in a follow-up question that fueled further inquiry and instructional change: "How aware are students of the way their thinking is helping them as they read?" What do you wonder about your students as readers? It may be useful to return to the discussion in Chapter 1 of Kucer's (2008) dimensions of reading (linguistic, cognitive, sociocultural, and developmental) to consider different ways you might inquire into your students' reading processes, habits, and attitudes.

The work of Richard and his classmates confirmed Stephanie's belief that she needed to continue modeling her own thinking as she read. Even more significantly, she knew she needed to talk more about when and how her observations and questions were helping her make sense of text. Because Richard and his classmates already displayed some ability to think more about their questions than about other types of responses, she had a clear sense of where to start in her attempt to support her students in the transition from being mere responders to being readers who are in control of how they are processing what they read.

This two-step sticky note activity was just a start to Stephanie's inquiry into what her students do when they read and how to help them improve comprehension. An inquiry approach to assessment is ongoing, with the teacher constantly seeking ways to better "operationalize" reading—to get kids to show what they're doing as they read. As the construct validity of the classroom-based assessment improves through teacher inquiry, so does the teacher's ability to know what to do next—which in turn ensures a higher degree of consequential validity. Assessment viewed through this lens is not something that *happens*; rather, it is constantly in process. Teachers taking this stance are either learning something new about their students as readers or taking stock of whether an instructional intervention was successful for a student.

Using Classroom-Based Assessment Information to Challenge Bad Ideas

At this point in her inquiry, Stephanie shared with me that some district administrators were calling into question some of her professional choices. The push to implement Response to Intervention (RTI) in high schools, well intentioned as it may be, was becoming a complicated struggle for Stephanie and some of her colleagues, as scholars such as William Brozo (2009) predicted it might. Specifically, predetermined interventions were getting all the attention, and consideration of the information necessary to determine the need for or appropriateness of an intervention was coming as an afterthought, if it came at all. Stephanie needed to justify why she wasn't implementing one of the five "research-based," district-approved interventions. Sadly, authentic guided reading, with its high reliance on teacher expertise and the need for flexibility in time and instructional resources, was not on the list. Her inquiry-based approach to assessment, with its goal of creating a better understanding of her students as readers in order to teach them more effectively, was at odds with the district-level approach, with its "focused attention on implementing specific curriculum programs [and] interventions" (SARW, p. 17), without the necessary attention to careful assessment.

The people who assembled this list of five interventions, who purchased some of the published materials, and who shipped them to Stephanie had not indicated what kinds of evidence she would need to gather to know which intervention was appropriate—to say nothing of the commensurate lack of professional development required to implement these interventions. In a bizarre twist on the SARW's central contention about the relationship between assessment and consequences, Stephanie was being asked to leap to "consequence"—systematized instructional response—without any thoughtful consideration of the assessment information that should lead her to one. Though the frustration Stephanie was feeling was intense and highly personal, I suspect her case is far from unique.

Many of Stephanie's students enter high school with a history of failure in reading and writing. They are precisely the kinds of kids the SARW refer to as those who are "initially less successful than others in literacy acquisition" and who "often find that their curriculum shrinks to one that is less engaging and less mind-expanding, . . . reducing the breadth and complexity of the literacy students acquire" (p. 21). Stephanie was, in fact, being pressured to abandon her approach in favor of a scripted reading program. She had been provided a single level of text for a comprehension program, purchased in the complete absence of assessment information about her students, and was expected to begin instructing students in comprehension with several selections about—a jar of mustard. Later, the program would have students reading a series of passages about a wealthy man who dreamed of taking a tropical vacation. These lessons were to be supplemented with occasional fluency drills and practice activities. This vastly shrunken curriculum, which had absolutely no potential to speak to her students' lives and interests, was not something Stephanie was prepared to deploy.

Consequently, Stephanie was even more determined to build on the inquiry approach to assessment in which she was already engaged to find out more about what her students could do and with what level of text. Her goals were now twofold: to improve her instruction and to communicate with administrators who were calling her practice into question. She found herself in a situation in which she knew she had to accept her "responsibility for making and sharing judgments about students' achievements and progress" and not "defer to others or to other instruments" to make instructional decisions (SARW, p. 14). To that end, we read and discussed Scott's (2008) "Assessing Text Processing: A Comparison of Four Methods," which concludes that teachers can get the most insight into their students'

Student think-alouds ask students to share insights about what they're reading and how they're reading it *as they read*. Kucan and Beck (1997) summarize their review of literature on thinking aloud and reading comprehension in this way: "The potential to reveal, which is the power of thinking aloud as a method of inquiry, is also an aspect of its potential as a method of instruction" (p. 292). Through the *inquiry aspect of thinking aloud,* feedback about student progress relative to the learning goals is made possible when teachers can gain access to students' thought processes as they read. The notion of the *think-aloud conceived as an instructional tool* aligns with the need to provide models of expert thinking as demonstrated by the teacher. Teacher-directed think-alouds receive more attention in Chapter 3.

reading processes by requesting that students think aloud while they read accessible text and answer some process-based interview questions after they read.

To facilitate this process, Stephanie selected first chapters of two books, Kate DiCamillo's *Because of Winn-Dixie* and Katherine Paterson's *The Bridge to Terabithia*, to allow for some differentiation of text difficulty. She marked each passage with four dark lines, splitting the chapter into roughly equal chunks indicating where students should stop to tell her what they were thinking. After they read, she asked each student a series of questions to try to gain a fuller picture of how they were processing text as they read.

Admittedly, these preparatory steps sound like a significant amount of work. Engaging in this process also meant that Stephanie would need to meet with each of her students one on one to perform the assessment (the luxuries of small class sizes and a volunteer tutor from the local university minimized the disruption to instruction). But these are the very considerations related to consequential validity I discussed earlier. When facing decisions such as whether the time required to construct and deliver an assessment as robust as this is worth it, it's useful for secondary teachers to keep in mind Paris's (2005) differentiation between *constrained* and *unconstrained* reading skills. Afflerbach (2011) interprets the distinction particularly well:

> In contrast [to reading skills such as letter-sound relationships], skills and strategies related to constructing meaning (comprehension and vocabulary) are less constrained. They typically take more time to assess. Questions and prompts related to reading comprehension assessment may have divergent, acceptable responses or performances. Higher-order thinking involves more unconstrained skills and strategies that contribute to reading for understanding. (p. 301)

So, although an inquiry approach to assessment doesn't by any means guarantee consequential validity, secondary teachers can be certain that the time it takes to dig for elements of "truth" about their students as readers is an integral, unavoidable part of the process. If we feel adolescent reading comprehension is important to know about, we have to set aside the time and space for this knowledge to develop. Some of this time will be "new" time devoted to assessment or analysis of student work, but much of it, done as part of the work of the content area classroom, requires no more than the time it takes for students to read and respond to well-selected text from the discipline.

Reading Assessment: Side by Side

In spite of the time investment required to prepare, Stephanie was ready to plunge wholeheartedly into this new assessment of think-alouds and after-reading questions. Using what she knew about Richard from assessments like the sticky note activity, Stephanie decided to use the passage from *The Bridge of Terabithia* to assess him. (Because one of the consequences of any assessment is the time it takes to administer and interpret it, looking for ways such as this to use assessment data to inform multiple decisions helps improve the validity of the assessment.) Richard decided to read aloud, allowing us to make some observations on the right in Figure 2.4; his comments from the think-aloud are on the left. Figure 2.5 shares the questions we asked afterward, adapted from Scott (2008), as well as Richard's answers. Not including up-front text preparation time, this process took about twenty-five minutes from start to finish and garnered a wealth of information far beyond any standardized data Stephanie had on Richard. For one, Stephanie confirmed that given fiction at this level of complexity, Richard could read independently with a fairly high degree of comprehension. More specifically, she was able to start compiling a list of strengths from which to build and areas of concern on which to focus:

> *Strengths:* Infers reasonably from details; displays incredulity at an unusual event (suggesting some metacognition); uses his own language to summarize accurately; shows an awareness of what to do if he encounters a word he doesn't know.

> *Weaknesses:* Ignores a text feature that is unfamiliar; low awareness of miscues; no sense of prereading behaviors such as predicting based on title, skimming, and so forth; frames difficulty of text on word level only

An added benefit of this method of assessment was Stephanie's ability to gain some insight into Richard's *affect* as a reader. His response to the question about inclination to continue reading is positive, but it was based on his sense that the story wasn't going to have anything to do with school. As we met with student after student and gained similar levels of insight (though naturally not always so positive), Stephanie shared this testament to the power of inquiry-based assessment: "I wish I had done this at the beginning of the year!"

Since working with Stephanie on this project, I've had the chance to collaborate with Sarah Walsh, who teaches another section of self-contained English. Because her class size is similarly manageable, we assessed her students on the first two days of the school year and set goals based on what we noticed. We used a similar assessment to look for growth midyear and will do so again at the end of the year. For small classes with students whose needs are quite intense, I recommend a process similar to this before beginning instruction. The examples from my own reading class in the sections to come might be more appropriate for larger classes.

Figure 2.4: Transcript of Richard's think-aloud during oral reading (left) and additional teacher observations during reading (on the right). *The Bridge to Terabithia* opens on a farm in the early morning, when Jess sneaks out of his house to go for a run through the cow pasture.

Richard's thoughts	Our observations as he read
Sounds like they're on a farm. Waking up. They're gonna get in trouble by their mama. They've gotta sneak out?	He skipped the opening lines, car noises in italics. He had lots of miscues on words.
The boy was practicing for school, to run every morning—he'd wake up. He had all these sisters. Only one them is not gonna dress him up.	
He was on a farm again. Someone was making breakfast. Sounds like he was talking to a cow! He was flying around a cow or something?	
The first day back at school, the upper kids get the advantages, the equipment. The boys run and the girls play hopscotch and talk.	Stumbled on *except*, replaced with *especially*, but didn't notice the shift in meaning it created.

Figure 2.5: Transcript of the questions we asked after the think-aloud (on the left) and Richard's answers (on the right).

What are some things you did to get ready to read?	Nothing.
Did you connect any of the ideas you thought of before reading to what you were reading at the time?	Nope.
While you were reading, did you come to anything that didn't make sense? What did you do?	No.
Did you come to any words you didn't know? What did you do?	Yeah, some of them. I tried to sound them out and make some guesses. Yeah, some.
Did anything surprise you about what you read?	No surprises.
What are some things you did when you finished reading?	I felt happy that I got it over with!
Do you think this chapter was too easy, too hard, or just about right? Why do you think so?	It was okay . . . a lot of the words I knew. Some chapter books be putting all them big words from the dictionary.
Tell us what this chapter was about.	A boy trying to get out of his house and go practice. He has to sneak out because his mama won't let him go out that early. Looks like he loves to run.
Would you keep reading this story? Why or why not?	Yeah, it seems good. 'Cause it's about nothing to do with school. It looks good.

Write It Down: The Power of Record-Keeping

As Stephanie and I talked through Richard's performance, we decided she needed to start formalizing her understanding of what her students could do. Even though additional paperwork is low on teacher's wish lists, Stephanie was eager to make a simple chart like the one in Figure 2.6 to begin collecting what she knew about her students. This activity, while again time-consuming, served a number of purposes. Foremost, it gave Stephanie a way of thinking about all the assessment she engages in all the time in her classroom and giving it a space to make it legitimate. Secondary teachers, I find, are likely to put the qualifier *only* in front of the words *an observation* or *observational*—as in "I know the kid can do that, but only from observation" or "My only evidence is observational. I don't have anything solid to back it up." The SARW empower teachers by reminding us that we "are in a unique position to engage in valid assessment. Because [we] are closest to students' learning, [we] have the opportunity to make many detailed observations over time" (p. 14). It's partly because of the number of students we see every day that we've been reduced to such dismissal of our powers of professional observation, a consequence of which is that we let our observations dissipate into the air of the crowded classroom. Such relinquishment of our own expertise is also related to the dominant ideology of "teachers' observations . . . as informal and subjective [in contrast to] test results that are considered 'formal' and 'objective'" (SARW, p. 9). For things we really care about, in times when they matter most, it's crucial to get those observations in writing, side by side with—and, I suggest, before—the kinds of information outsiders prize.

Figure 2.6: A record-keeping tool that privileges teacher observational data alongside standardized assessment results.

Student Name	Informal Assessment/ Observational Data	Formal/Standardized Assessment Information	Possible Instructional Responses
Richard	Goes back to text when looking for answers, uses context clues and sounding out when faced with unknown words. Good at predictions. Volunteers to read in class, reads more than one paragraph.	Think-aloud/Interview: with 5th grade level narrative text—making strong inferences, sometimes using sophisticated vocabulary, good comprehension, lots of miscues. Given 3-1 Easy CBM 15/20 in comprehension. Reads 112 wpm at the 4th- grade level according to CBM data.	Increase exposure to high-frequency vocabulary, more access to authentic text at instructional level (4th grade).

Putting all of this information in writing, organized with student names first and instructional response last, also helped Stephanie communicate an important message to the administrators who were asking her to deploy scripted intervention curricula: carefully gathered information and inferences derived about students from assessments *have* to be the cornerstone of decision making. In our efforts to implement quick fixes and meet externally mandated levels of proficiency, processes that take time and professional expertise can get glossed over in the service of getting an intervention in place, fast. The result is that even well-intentioned adults who daily talk the talk of putting students first can make poor decisions when they are under pressure to get a program in place to create the appearance of action.

Stephanie's work as an assessor might be summed up in a clear definition of assessment from Genishi and Dyson (2009), whose work with younger learners and readers I admire immensely. Assessment, they suggest, is "an ongoing, complex process in which we aim to discover and document what children are learning over time in many situations and across multiple symbol systems, so that we can help them learn more" (p. 116). Though Stephanie's inquiry did not involve varying symbol systems (her concern was work with alphabetic text), her questions drove her to look for tools that allowed her to uncover information she could formalize through documentation. Through study of that documentation, she could consider adjustments in instruction to help students like Richard read and learn more effectively. The process is neither perfect nor easy, but there is no substitute for it (see Figure 2.7).

Reading Assessment as Organic Outgrowth of Curriculum

At the time I was working with teachers on this project, I was, like Stephanie, teaching a yearlong reading support class for high school students but with students who received no other special services. When I began teaching the course in 2009, course-alike teachers from our area high schools met with our district curriculum coordinator to discuss curriculum and student selection. Though assessment was not officially on the agenda, this meeting called attention to the fact that assessment was absolutely central to any decisions we would be making. In fact, the frustration and confusion that grew out of that meeting caused me, quite by accident, to begin thinking about this course with assessment at its center. Afflerbach (2011) reminds us that

> too often, assessment operates from a top-down position, and tests drive curriculum; or assessment represents a series of afterthoughts—added to an instructional program because it is required, and not because it is tightly aligned with teaching goals and student learning. Optimally, assessment is seamless with teaching and learning, and it develops organically with curriculum. (p. 311)

Figure 2.7: Carefully considering the relationships between instructional responses and assessment tools.

In the record-keeping chart Stephanie created, she was intentional about the rhetoric of the order of the columns: Student name, What she knows about students, What instructional responses (district mandated and her own) might be appropriate. The reasons for doing so are implied in Stephanie's situation, but that is not by any means the only way to think about or visually represent the relationships between students, assessment, and instruction.

You'll see other examples in this book that look more like this:

Probable instructional response	Assessment tool to facilitate differentiation	Student groupings
High-, average-, low-difficulty readings to build background knowledge on new content topic	Teacher knowledge about student reading level, informed by state testing data; student responses to anticipation guide on upcoming content	High difficulty Average difficulty Low difficulty

The order in which you think about students, assessment tools, and instructional response should be flexible and determined by context—but it should be done with intention. Generally speaking, the closer you are to the daily interactions of students, the more you can think like the chart in this graphic. After all, since those closest to students—the teachers who teach them—are those responsible for acting on classroom assessment, having possible instructional responses in mind *as the reason for deploying an assessment* is fairly key to maximizing consequential validity.

The following classroom example demonstrates my attempts to establish those optimal assessment conditions for my students—not because I was conscious of meeting some sort of research-based standard, but simply because I needed to know what to teach.

Using a fairly sophisticated data management program, our curriculum coordinator pulled up and manipulated color-coded dots that represented all the ninth graders who would be attending each of the high schools. Then we focused on kids who scored below or at the low end our state's eighth-grade assessment "meets" level. Knowing that "the more consequential the decision, the more important it is to seek diverse perspectives and independent sources of data" (SARW, p. 24), we factored in students' scores on a pre-ACT test with a predictive relationship to the state high school exam. Finally, from this pool of students, we factored *out* any student who received any other special support services.

Through standardized assessment measures and a data-sorting process reminiscent of the high-tech world in the science fiction film *Minority Report*, we created a group of students who seemed to have something in common. But what that "thing" in common was—and what implications it had for course design or immediate instructional steps—eluded us. We could not even begin to deduce grade-level proficiency despite having the entirety of these students' official school records literally at our fingertips. The wisdom of the SARW's warning about the futility of using multiple, though similarly narrow, forms of assessment to aid in inquiry and problem solving could not have been clearer (p. 25).

Recall that inquiry-focused assessment centers on questions that help you know your students better as readers and thinkers. Ideally, you'll have some potential instructional responses already in mind when you give the assessment, but when you're first getting started, as I was, this might not be possible. Bear in mind that if the assessment result is that you have a better mental construct of your students as readers and thinkers, this is a considerable achievement that will play out in instruction even if you're not initially aware of it.

During this meeting, we also developed a basic instructional framework for the class, agreeing that it would involve lots of teacher modeling of effective reading habits with authentic texts. The habits we would focus on would include

- Setting a purpose for reading
- Activating prior knowledge
- Using prior knowledge to make high- and low-level inferences
- Determining what's important
- Asking questions to check for understanding and fuel new understanding
- Varying reading rate and strategy based on the reader's level of understanding

With such a curricular focus in place, I set about designing an assessment that would help me answer the following set of inquiry questions I had about the nebulously "similar" students who would be enrolled in my class:

- Am I in the ballpark on independent reading level? (We were theoretically choosing students who were reading two to three grades below grade level.)
- How do these students respond to questions that mirror the habits of effective readers?
- How well can they articulate their thinking while they read?

Getting into Their Heads

The assessment model I developed—and now use variations of routinely as the centerpiece of my reading instruction—consisted of eight questions, a passage I adapted from an ancillary social studies text, a prompt to promote active reading, and plenty of marginal space in which students could share their thinking. For the purposes of this task, I excerpted a passage about Martin Luther King Jr., and constructed a title ("Dr. King Gets a Prize and Goes to Jail") that I was confident would universally allow students to tap into something they knew about a figure from history. On the first sheet, students were asked to consider this context:

Imagine that in your American history class your teacher asks you to read independently a brief article called "Dr. King Gets a Prize and Goes to Jail." After you read the article, you'll be asked to explain some of its main ideas to a friend.

Students then wrote in response to two prereading questions:

What do you think you might already know about an article from an American history class called "Dr. King Gets a Prize and Goes to Jail?"

What do you expect to learn or find out by reading this article?

Only after students responded to these questions did I distribute the reading passage. The active reading prompt asked them to read carefully the text in the left-hand column and to share anything they were thinking in the right-hand column. Because this assessment's goal was to help me understand students' current ability to articulate their thinking as they read, I offered no modeling or examples and was intentionally vague on this point. If students asked whether a certain type of response was appropriate (e.g., "Can I ask questions?"), I assured them that anything that showed me what they were thinking as they read would be helpful to me.

> These questions exemplify attempts to bolster the assessment's construct validity. If we know that effective readers set purposes for their reading—and that they need an active set of prior knowledge on which to build new meaning as they read—I needed to see what they were able to do with prompts that elicit such information. Because these habits and skills were also agreed-upon curricular goals, this kind of assessment was neatly aligned all around.

When students finished reading the passage and annotating their thinking, I followed up with six more questions on separate paper. I have included them here with parenthetical commentary suggesting what I was trying to find out in relation to the course's curricular goals and the specific goals of this assessment:

- You've been asked to share a summary of this article with a friend. What would you tell him or her? (Overall comprehension; Determining what's important; Is this text too hard?)

- After reading the article, what do you still want to know? What are you curious about? (Asking good questions; Intellectual curiosity)

- Was there any place in the article where you got lost or confused? What did you do to try to make sense of what you were reading? (Self-awareness; Use of fix-up strategies)

- Look back at your predictions and expectations from the first page of this activity. Did you learn what you expected to learn? Explain. (Evaluating success in light of purposes set)

- What did you like about reading this article? What did you not like? (Affective awareness)

- Is there anything else you would like to share about this article or how you read it? (General: Acknowledging students may have something to say that's unrelated to the questions I thought were important)

Looking at Student Work

Before you see how some of my students responded to the course preassessment, I need to get a little ahead of myself to share some thoughts about examining student work. I'm in complete agreement with the SARW that "ensuring that assessment leads to the improvement of teaching and learning is not simply a technical matter of devising instruments for generating higher quality data" (p. 16). The assessment I designed and the information I gleaned from it were absolutely necessary for improving the instruction I provided, but merely possessing the information wasn't enough. The following three conditions were crucial in allowing me to use the information gathered through inquiry-based assessment to improve instruction:

- Allowing myself the time to examine the work carefully
- Having an instructional framework that allows response through full-class, small-group, and independent instruction in place (more on this in Chapter 3)
- Committing substantial amounts of class time to the acts of reading and writing in order to see these processes occurring on a daily basis

Central to that connection between the well-constructed assessment instrument and thoughtfully designed instruction, then, is determining a way to think through the work you'll be examining. The most common way of doing this is through a rubric, or a listing of desired characteristics and performance levels that describe levels of proficiency relative to them.

When I began teaching this course, I was hesitant to use such a rigid instrument and avoided anything that tried to quantify performance in the different domains. I used a document similar to Figure 2.8 that simply lists the desired observable behaviors in one column and leaves space for me to describe the student work in the other. I found this useful in developing an understanding of what each performance assessment was telling me, but not very helpful for detecting individual student progress from one assessment to the next, and it wasn't useful information for students.

The next time I gave such an assessment, I shifted approaches to one that identified certain products, processes, and habits of mind I was investigating and that described four levels of performance (see Figure 2.9). This second version is useful for seeing growth over time—for both me and my students (the students are curious about those charts with numbers)—although it cannot account for issues such as increased text complexity, which makes cross-assessment comparisons challenging. As I share some of my impressions of student work related to the preassessment previously described, you may wish to look at one or both of the instruments (Figures 2.8 and 2.9) I provide to start thinking through the students' responses. First I look at the responses of three students (Maria, John, and Davon)

Figure 2.8: A first attempt to look for evidence of valued habits in student reading assessment, with sample annotations.

Habit	Evidence of Habit
Activate and effectively use prior knowledge to create meaning	*Wrote three facts about MLK, but wasn't able to show connections between these facts and what she read.*
Ask varied and relevant questions to clarify understanding	*A few insightful questions; one showed a connection between question, answer, and comprehension.*
Determine what is important	*Summary touches on main idea, but is more of a retelling.*
Draw high-level and low-level inferences during and after reading	*No evidence*
Expand vocabulary knowledge and use	*No evidence—Did ask "What does this mean?"*
Self-monitor and engage in fix-up strategies	*Realization that question had been answered*

to the prereading questions, asking them to generate background knowledge and make some purpose-setting predictions (see Figures 2.10–2.12). Then I look at Maria's and Davon's annotations and postreading questions (Figures 2.13 and 2.14).

As you examine students' responses to the prereading questions, you might notice something similar to my observations, summarized here:

Maria: Accurately inferred "Dr. King" to be MLK and called up two facts about him; offered more generalized belief about MLK, noting that he "didn't give up." She explicitly draws on her knowledge of story structure to predict that she will discover a problem and a resolution, mapping the specifics of her knowledge of MLK onto it: "I'm thinking that going to jail might be a problem that later results in him winning the prize."

John: Offers up less information about his thinking, and though his purposes for reading are just as accurate as Maria's, he seems to rely heavily on the language of the prompt (the title) for his own responses.

Davon: In contrast to Maria, who accurately associated "Dr. King" with MLK, and John, who offered no insight on his thinking, Davon misidentifies "Dr. King" and creates a story line about theft of a prize that leads to imprisonment. He does, however, set reasonable cognitive purposes for reading.

Figure 2.9: A second tool I used to examine student assessments for information.

	Product: Summary
4	The student summarizes the article very effectively, including an understanding of main idea and some significant details, expressed articulately in the student's own words. Meaningful extensions, comparisons, or connections may be integrated as well.
3	The student summarizes the article effectively, identifying a plausible main idea and relating some details, most of which are relevant and significant. The student may rely on language from the article and likely makes no extension beyond the text.
2	The student overrelies on retelling, making only limited attempts at differentiating between a central idea and details.
1	The student offers a summary that reveals significant lack of comprehension.

	Product: Activating and Using Prior Knowledge
4	The student activates significant, specific prior knowledge before reading and clearly articulates its usefulness in comprehending text during and/or after reading.
3	The student activates specific prior knowledge before reading and makes attempts at articulating its usefulness in comprehending during and/or after reading.
2	The student activates some prior knowledge but shows little ability to connect it to comprehension during and/or after reading.
1	The student shows little ability to activate prior knowledge.

	Process: Stating a Purpose for Reading
4	The student articulates a clear and meaningful purpose for reading the text based on the information known from the prompt and title.
3	The student suggests a reasonable purpose for reading, but may not relate it directly to the information known from the prompt.
2	The student suggests a purpose that is unclear or underdeveloped.
1	The student is unable to suggest a purpose for reading.

	Habit of Mind: Curiosity
4	The student reveals significant interest in something still—or new—to be learned based on the content of the reading.
3	The student suggests interest in something yet to be learned, but may not connect it directly to content in the reading.
2	The student suggests an unclear or underdeveloped notion of something yet to be learned.
1	The student is unable to suggest an area of further curiosity.

	Process: Metacognition
4	The student reveals an awareness of a broad and abundant range of comprehension-related thinking such as questioning, connecting, clarifying, and inferring—nearly all of which seem to contribute to understanding.
3	The student reveals an awareness of a range of comprehension-related thinking, much of which seems to contribute to understanding.
2	The student reveals an awareness of some comprehension-related thinking, though the variety may be limited and some may seem unrelated to understanding.
1	The student reveals little awareness of comprehension-related thinking, and what is revealed may seem unrelated to understanding.

Figure 2.10: Maria's responses to the prereading questions.

In your social studies class, the teacher asks you to read independently a brief article called "Dr. King Gets a Prize and Goes to Jail." After you read the article, you'll be asked to explain some of its main ideas to a friend.

First: What do you think you might already know about an article from American history class called "Dr. King Gets a Prize and Goes to Jail'? List this prior knowledge here. (As you are reading, you might write a note next to any part in the article where you use your prior knowledge to understand the article.)

- Martin Luther King the "I have a dream" speech in Washington, D.C.

- Martin Luther King won the Noble Peace Prize.

- Martin Luther King didn't give up.

Second: What do you expect to learn or find out by reading this article?

In this article, you should be able to figure out what the climax is. You should be able to find out a problem and later on a resolution. I'm thinking that going to jail might be a problem that later results in him winning the prize.

Figure 2.11: John's responses to the prereading questions.

In your social studies class, the teacher asks you to read independently a brief article called "Dr. King Gets a Prize and Goes to Jail." After you read the article, you'll be asked to explain some of its main ideas to a friend.

First: What do you think you might already know about an article from a social studies class called "Dr. King Gets a Prize and Goes to Jail"? List this prior knowledge here. (As you are reading, you might write a note next to any part in the article where you use your prior knowledge to understand the article.)

- Dr, king gets a Prize that got him in Jail,
- we are reading it in Soc. Studys

Second: What do you expect to learn or find out by reading this article?

- What the prize is.
- why he went to Jail

Figure 2.12: Davon's responses to the prereading questions.

In your social studies class, the teacher asks you to read independently a brief article called "Dr. King Gets a Prize and Goes to Jail." After you read the article, you'll be asked to explain some of its main ideas to a friend.

First: What do you think you might already know about an article from a social studies class called "Dr. King Gets a Prize and Goes to Jail"? List this prior knowledge here. (As you are reading, you might write a note next to any part in the article where you use your prior knowledge to understand the article.)

I think it's about a king getting something but he stole It but then again he thought It was his prize but then later on that day he got caught with the prize

Second: What do you expect to learn or find out by reading this article?

I expect to find out what the prize was and to see why he went to Jail

Moments such as these reveal the complex in-
terrelationships between assessment, instruction, and content knowledge and expertise.
What is heartening about these connections is
that building teacher capacity with one leads
to development in the others. You don't have to
(and cannot) wait until you can claim expertise
in all three areas—reading, reading assessment, and the content you're teaching—before
starting to use authentic, performance-based
reading assessment with adolescents.

If one of my purposes for this preassessment was to
find out more about what is going on in students'
minds as they read, you can already see its usefulness.
If, however, I hoped to readily see patterns of behavior
that imply instructional responses appropriate for the
entire class (or even for considerable portions of the
class), this assessment is not as immediately useful.

As I continue to look at how students responded
to the preasssessment, I narrow the cases down to
those of Maria (Figure 2.13) and Davon (Figure 2.14;
he made no annotations on the second page), both of
whom set reasonable purposes for reading, but who
brought with them very different kinds of background
knowledge. Notice that the marginal comments in Maria's assessment all rely heavily on the observation she made in the first part of the task (Figure 2.10): "Martin
Luther King didn't give up." It's difficult to tell whether specific textual content is
prompting some of her responses as she continues to develop the central theme she
indicated as prior knowledge. On the second page of her responses, she takes up
Malcolm X as a new topic, but she folds him in with her treatment of MLK rather
than noticing that the text is actually seeking to portray them as different ("Both
King and Malcolm X believed in integration and that blacks and whites shouldn't
be seperated").

Though it causes Maria to miss out on some of the subtlety of the passage,
her activated prior knowledge seems to support her comprehension of the text.
If her prior knowledge had been less fully developed (or less accurate), however,
would Maria have had the ability to adjust to what the text was telling her? Davon
provides a sense of what I mean. Recall that he predicted from the title that this
passage would be about "a king," not Martin Luther King. In a way, his marginal
comments in Figure 2.14 reveal a higher degree of engagement with the specifics
of the text than do Maria's. Sometimes he's restating, sometimes clarifying an understanding; sometimes he's evaluating or inferring. He doesn't note any confusion
about his prediction relating to a member of a royal family—until, when prompted
to reflect on his predictions in the postreading activity, he points out the he "had
no idea this was going to be about MLK." Like Maria, Davon doesn't make any
note of Malcolm X serving as a figure of contrast to King.

A look at my impressions of their postreading responses side by side (see
Figure 2.15) offers further insight into what these two very different readers did
with the same piece of text. Certainly, Maria and Davon are showing me that
regardless of any numerical similarities between tests they took in the past (and in
fact their eighth-grade standardized test scores are one number apart on a scale of

Figure 2.13: Maria's during-reading annotations (middle column) and responses to follow-up questions (right-hand column).

Text of article	Your thoughts as you read	
Dr. King Gets a Prize and Goes to Jail		You've been asked to **share a summary** of this article with a friend. What would you tell him or her? This article is basically about how Martin Luther King J.r. was determined to fight for what he believed in no matter what happend.
Martin Luther King, Jr., was in the hospital. He wasn't seriously ill; it was a case of exhaustion. It was Tuesday and he'd given three speeches on Sunday and two on Monday. And there were all those trips to jail, and the marches, and the pressures. But when the phone rang, he felt a whole lot better. Matter of fact, he felt great.	Martin Luther King was a very confident man. Martin Luther King was willing to sacrifice for what he believed in.	
His wife, Coretta, had big news: Martin had been awarded the Nobel Peace Prize. That prize is given each year to the person, from anywhere in the world, who has contributed most to peace. Martin Luther King, Jr., at 35, was the youngest person ever to receive it.		After reading the article, what do you **still want to know**? What are you curious about? There's nothing I'm curious about.
Some Americans were furious, and they wrote to the Nobel committee in Sweden and told them so. Bull Connor said, "They're scraping the bottom of the barrel." But most Americans were proud. Newspaper columnist Ralph McGill, writing in the *Atlanta Constitution*, said Europeans understood King better than most Americans. They saw in him "the American promise," with its message for the whole world.	Even though people were upset, he was still confident.	Was there any place in the article where you **got lost or confused**? What did you do to try to make sense of what you were reading? No, there wasn't but if there was I would re-read until I understand.
King flew to Europe to receive the Peace Prize. He invited his parents, his wife, and 25 friends to go with him. The Nobel chairman awarded him the Prize and said that King was "the first person in the Western world to have shown us that a struggle can be waged without violence."		
He was soon back in America and in jail again. He was in Selma, Alabama, trying to help black citizens vote. Martin Luther King, Jr., marched with 250 citizens who wanted to register to vote. They were all thrown in jail. King, too.	Martin Luther King Jr went to jail and still, that didn't stop him.	Look back at **your predictions and expectations** from the first page of this activity. Did you learn what you expected to learn? Explain. I didn't learn anything new, I basically knew all the information the text had to offer.
When they heard of Dr. King's arrest, 500 schoolchildren marched to the courthouse. They were arrested. Two days later 300 more schoolchildren were arrested. The evening television news covered it all.		
King wrote a letter from jail. He said, "This is Selma, Alabama. There are more Negroes in jail with me than there are on the voting rolls. Fifteen congressmen came to Selma. They announced that "new legislation is going to be necessary." President Johnson held a press conference and said, "All Americans should be indignant when one American is denied the right to vote."		What did you **like** about reading this article? What did you **not like**? I didn't like reading this article because it was to simple and I already knew everything in the article.
Coretta Scott King went to the jail to visit her husband. She brought a message from Malcolm X, who was also in Selma. Malcolm, a black leader who was electrifying urban audiences with hard facts and a spirit of militancy, had been invited to Selma by black leaders. His ideas were different from King's. Malcolm had never recognized the power and force of nonviolent action. But Malcolm seemed to be heading in a new direction. He told Coretta, "I want Dr. King to know that I didn't come to Selma to make his job difficult." Then he added, "If the white people realize what the alternative is, perhaps they will be more willing to hear Dr. King."	Both King and Malcom X believed in integration. blacks and whites shoulan't be seperated	Is there **anything else** you would like to share about this article or how you read it? It was really short and easy not really interesting.
The alternative was violence. Speaking to a big crowd at a church in Selma, Malcolm said, "White people should thank Dr. King for holding people in check, for there are others who do not believe in these nonviolent measures."		

Figure 2.14: Davon's during-reading annotations (middle column) and responses to follow-up questions (right-hand column).

Text of article	Your thoughts as you read	

Dr. King Gets a Prize and Goes to Jail

Martin Luther King, Jr., was in the hospital. He wasn't seriously ill; it was a case of exhaustion. It was Tuesday and he'd given three speeches on Sunday and two on Monday. And there were all those trips to jail, and the marches, and the pressures. But when the phone rang, he felt a whole lot better. Matter of fact, he felt great.

His wife, Coretta, had big news: Martin had been awarded the Nobel Peace Prize. That prize is given each year to the person, from anywhere in the world, who has contributed most to peace. Martin Luther King, Jr., at 35, was the youngest person ever to receive it.

Some Americans were furious, and they wrote to the Nobel committee in Sweden and told them so. Bull Connor said, "They're scraping the bottom of the barrel." But most Americans were proud. Newspaper columnist Ralph McGill, writing in the *Atlanta Constitution*, said Europeans understood King better than most Americans. They saw in him "the American promise," with its message for the whole world.

King flew to Europe to receive the Peace Prize. He invited his parents, his wife, and 25 friends to go with him. The Nobel chairman awarded him the Prize and said that King was "the first person in the Western world to have shown us that a struggle can be waged without violence."

He was soon back in America—and in jail again. He was in Selma, Alabama, trying to help black citizens vote. Martin Luther King, Jr., marched with 250 citizens who wanted to register to vote. They were all thrown in jail. King, too.

Handwritten annotations (middle column):

He was exhausted because he gave all those speeches

He went to jail because he was doing the right thing and the whites thought it was wrong

I think he got that award because he was making an change in the world.

I think a lot of people were gald MLK was getting even rights

It was good that king was awarded because he's one of a kind

whites didn't want stuff to get better

Right-hand column (responses to follow-up questions):

You've been asked to s hare a summary of this article with a friend. What would you tell him or her?

I would tell them that Martin Luther King, Jr was a great man with lots of thought and doing the things in an non-violent way

After reading the article, what do you still want to know? What are you curious about?

Why didn't Coretta Scott king take over for her husband when he was murdered

Was there any place in the article where you got lost or confused? What did you do to try to make sense of what you were reading?

I was confused when Bull Connor said; "they're scraping the bottom of the barrel." I didn't understand it at all

Look back at your predictions and expectations from the first page of this activity. Did you learn what you expected to learn? Explain.

No, I had no idea this was going to be about MLK

What did you like about reading this article? What did you not like?

I liked that the blacks finally got what they deserved and that was freedom and I didn't like how the blacks kept on getting thrown into jail for no reason

Is there anything else you would like to share about this article or how you read it?

I would like to share that MLK will never be forgotten

28), they approach text and make meaning of text—or at least this particular text—in significantly different ways. But partly because I selected text that, by traditional readability measures, was within their independent reading level (as best I could guess), they were able to demonstrate a definite ability to think about text as they read it. One of the flaws of standardized reading tests used for accountability purposes is that, by design, at least half the students at that grade level are not able to fully access the text.

It's important to note here that what I looked for in assessing the work that students produced was inextricably linked to possible instructional responses. To return to the SARW's central notion of the role of assessment in improving instruction, having potential instructional responses of frameworks in mind (think-alouds and small-group and individual conferences—I discuss this model explicitly in Chapter 3) allows teachers to get the most out of assessment. Part of the "assessment as inquiry" paradigm (Serafini, 2000–2001) implies that action will occur as a result of quality assessment.

I certainly had no idea where the students' responses would tell me I needed to go instructionally, but knowing that I had the tools of full-class think-alouds, small response groups during collaborative learning time, and individual conferences during independent reading made me confident I could *do something* with the assessment information. I contrast this to the way I taught English early in my career, when I relied almost exclusively on full-class discussion or completion of

Figure 2.15: Summary of how Maria and Davon responded to the follow-up questions.

Prompt	Maria	Davon
Share a summary	An accurate statement about MLK, but it reveals no understanding related to the content of the passage itself.	Makes a general statement about MLK and offers the detail of his nonviolent stance.
Still want to know?	No substantive response.	Asks a question about MLK's legacy through his wife.
Deal with confusion?	No, but offers rereading strategy as a possible response	Points out a moment in the text that was unclear, offers no insight into how he dealt with it.
Reflect on prior knowledge	Claims no new knowledge resulted from reading.	Clarified that he didn't realize it would be about MLK.
Like/not like	Expresses dislike because it was simple and offered nothing new.	Positive feelings toward the hopeful nature of the content, negative feelings toward the setbacks it discussed.
Anything else?	Short, not interesting.	"MLK will never be forgotten."

questions in small groups as the modes of instruction. In those modes, students were responding to my questions rather than the more productive arrangement of *me* responding to the information students offered up about their needs as developing readers.

Maria's and Davon's work implied for me a variety of instructional cues:

- In full-class think-alouds, I needed to show students how an effective reader makes use of background knowledge, both when the text confirms it and especially when the text disconfirms it. Students benefit most from think-alouds when a proficient reader demonstrates both success and frustration with text (Silvén & Vauras, 1992). For example, I shared with students my experience of beginning to read Jeannette Walls's memoir *The Glass Castle*. Because I expected the opening pages to be about the young girl whose story is told in the book, I had to work through a self-generated confusion when the opening chapter introduced the narrator as an adult, and I showed students how I did that.

- It's possible that Davon's reference to nonviolence in his summary might prompt Maria to notice that she glossed over the contrast with Malcolm X. In a small-group setting, these two students might work together to construct a summary that includes a high-level main idea statement and key relevant details.

- In one-on-one conferences, I can use text structure language with Maria to show her how I use that knowledge to navigate through text. With Davon, I may need to introduce the idea of text structure first before demonstrating how it can help him make sense of text.

My students take one of these assessments every six weeks or so as a natural extension of the unit we're studying. Using a similar format, I select a text that allows students to apply their knowledge developed over the course of the unit to respond to the process questions. For example, after reading Richard Wright's short novel *Rite of Passage*, students are assessed using a short excerpt from his

---

Though my inclination is to ask you to wait until you read about a teacher delivering a think-aloud in Chapter 3 to discuss them further, I understand that if you're not familiar with preparing and teaching with think-alouds, you may be a little frustrated at this point. Think-alouds, as I use them, are a way to respond to what I learn about students from their annotations. When I see a pattern of productive or unproductive thought, I use a short excerpt—usually a few paragraphs—to show them how I think as I read. To prepare, I either find the text online or type it into a document; doing so familiarizes me with the text *and* keeps me from selecting too long a chunk. Then I think about how I make sense of the text while I read, often focusing on some habit I want students to develop, such as moving beyond questioning to making thoughtful inferences. I use the Review tab to write out my thoughts in the margin so that the think-aloud is tightly planned. On the day of the think-aloud, I project the unaltered text on the overhead and use a printout with my marginal notes as an unofficial script.

autobiography, *Black Boy*. After reading the Young Readers Edition of *The Om-nivore's Dilemma*, students read and respond to a few pages of the introduction to another of Michael Pollan's books. Asking students to bring their developed knowledge about style, content, and ideas into a new, but not completely unfamiliar, setting is an activity they respond well to, even when the text is significantly more challenging, as in the case of the not-adapted-for-young-readers second book by Michael Pollan.

I should also add that in combination with the process-oriented questions and prompts I use to assess my students, I do sometimes construct more traditional multiple-choice comprehension/response items and include them as part of the assessment. I have to remind myself that, as useful as I find the more authentic student work, forced-choice questioning is part of students' real assessment experience, and it does offer a way of getting students to respond to aspects of the text that perhaps they wouldn't if not required to do so. Take, for example, verbalizing the philosophical differences between Martin Luther King Jr. and Malcolm X from the assessment discussed earlier. It would have been useful to know whether students had picked up on the differences because the absence of annotations on the subject doesn't necessarily mean an absence of understanding.

So far the portraits of inquiry-based reading assessment I've shared have come from classes in which the processes of reading comprehension are the content of the class. Knowing that this is neither the norm nor, truth be told, the ideal situation for students to develop critical comprehension that will serve them in a variety of disciplines, I close this chapter with examples of assessment-centered instruction from a biology and a world literature class. Though the teachers' stances as assessors vary considerably, both instructors sought information about how their students were developing as readers as a seamless part of their content area instruction, and both exemplify the power of assessment with strong construct and consequential validity.

"Try the hardest you can—I will help you through it"

This is what Faith Sharp told her students in her accelerated biology class as she passed back work at the beginning of the period. Students had recently written up the results of their inquiry into proteins in milk, their first lab report of high school, and Faith was offering verbal and written feedback carefully crafted to prompt revision and refine students' understanding of the conventions of writing in the academic discipline of science. Despite Faith's assurance that she would guide them through the process, one student inquired about grades. "I'm not concerned about grades right now," replied Faith. "I'm concerned about helping you learn how to do this."

Faith's sophisticated notion of assessment—as a process that privileges low-risk learning opportunities and feedback that prompts learning—was an approach students were just getting used to. And Faith was still getting used to her students as she gauged what they were able to do as writers, thinkers, and readers in her discipline. Knowing already that her students came from a variety of academic backgrounds and had diverse levels of skill and interest in her subject area, Faith wanted to learn more about her students as readers of science. So, as half of her students were engaged in an investigation into the behavior of guppies in tanks situated around her room, Faith started inquiring into her students' abilities and dispositions as science readers.

Her process began with carefully selected text, a relatively brief excerpt from *Reason for Hope* by Jane Goodall that describes Goodall's observation of chimpanzees using tools (see the left-hand column of Figure 2.16). Faith formatted this passage to allow a column for student responses, and while half the class visited the tanks to observe and take notes on guppies for half the period, the other half of the class read the text and wrote their responses to what they were reading. Then the students swapped tasks, and Faith had a sample of student work that she was eager to examine.

Faith read the students' responses and provided written feedback that honored their thoughts as genuine acts of communication—answering questions where appropriate, commenting on insights, and countering with her own questions to probe further thinking. She sensed that some students were already fairly adept at reading science, those who noticed the features of Goodall's text that discussed her scientific process, drew conclusions about the evidence she presented, and asked questions that demonstrated curiosity about her discoveries and methods. Other students, however, made significantly fewer comments overall, relied more heavily on restatement, and asked only superficial or tangentially related questions. Faith had already gotten a feel for which students likely had the background knowledge and dispositions as readers to handle some of the assignments she'd ask students to read; now she needed a plan to begin supporting those who indicated they might not be so ready.

When Faith and I met to review the student work, we decided we could use some of the stronger student responses to construct a sample set of annotations (see the right-hand column of Figure 2.16) that I would then deliver as a modified think-aloud. Doing so would give students further supportive feedback on the kind of thinking that meets the task of successfully navigating authentic science writing, offer models to students who were not yet performing at that level, and allow us to talk about how reading about science could help students learn about not only *the content* of the science but also the processes and intellectual stances that are central to the discipline.

Figure 2.16: Collected student responses delivered as a think-aloud.

While it was rare for a whole day to pass without at least one chimpanzee sighting, sometimes I had to wait hours and hours for the privilege. It was very important, during those periods of waiting, to stay watchful, because the chimpanzees were often in small groups, or even alone, and completely silent. It was the movement in a tree or the snapping of a branch that would alert me—though as often as not it would turn out to be baboons or monkeys and not chimps at all. One scientist who visited me during those early months was surprised that I did not take a supply of books up to the Peak, so that I could while away the hours of waiting. How much I would have missed!

I think that Jane Goodall has some serious patience, waiting for hours. She's not even promised the sight of *one* chimpanzee.

If you wait patiently you can get more out of a day than if you bring stuff to occupy your mind with.

During those days on the Peak I gradually began to piece together something of the daily life of the Gombe chimpanzees, and my fear of failure began to subside. But three months had passed before I made the first really significant and tremendously exciting observation. It had been a frustrating morning. I had tramped up and down three different valleys in search of chimps but had found none. At noon, weary from crawling through the dense undergrowth, I headed for the Peak. I stopped when I saw a dark shape and a slight movement in the long grass about forty yards ahead. Quickly focusing my binoculars, I saw that it was a single chimpanzee, and soon recognized the adult male, less fearful than the others, whom I already knew by sight. I had named him David Greybeard because of the distinctive white hair on his chin.

She obviously had devoted much time to this observation of chimps. Spending whole days without seeing a chimp is all made okay with just one sighting. She is easily able to recognize an already named chimp. She really cares about them.

I moved a little, so I could see him better. He was sitting on the red-earth mound of a termite nest, repeatedly pushing a grass stem into a hole. After a moment he would withdraw it, carefully, and pick something off with his mouth. Occasionally he picked a new piece of grass and used that. When he left I went over to the termite heap. Abandoned grass stems were scattered around. Termites were crawling about on the surface of the nest, already working to close up the openings into which David had poked his grasses. I tried doing as he had done, and when I pulled out my grass termites were clinging to it with their jaws.

I am sure Jane kept good records of times like these.

I don't know how she can be so amazed by chimpanzees eating termites with leaves. She went through that much trouble just to see that?

For students who demonstrated less proficiency in interacting with the text, Faith also wrote a quick note that she posted to their work (teachers can use sticky notes, too!), encouraging them to move beyond restatement, to try asking questions, or to make evaluations about the content they were reading. She kept a list of these students and her own comments so that she could remind herself to look for changes or growth in student responses as the year progressed. Although Faith knows that her job isn't to become a reading teacher, she realizes that her students will be more successful in her class if she calls attention to the kinds of reading behaviors that will serve them best and offers them the necessary support to develop those behaviors. This relatively simple process helps her do that—and her students are being exposed to key ideas and figures in the field of biology every time she does so.

Looking Ahead to Chapter 3: Systematic Formative Assessment

Students in Liz Dietz's sophomore English class were reading George Orwell's *Animal Farm*. One of the curricular objectives she and her course-alike teachers had agreed on was to help students develop an understanding of the language of propaganda. Liz knew she would need to provide some direct instruction in terminology (e.g., *loaded language*, *begging the question*), but she wanted the need for those terms to arise from students' interpretations of the text. She also wanted to create some flexible groups for a series of activities that she would carefully design to build understanding and independence with the novel—and the rhetorical devices of propaganda.

Through work we had done together, Liz's students were already accustomed to annotating text to demonstrate their thinking as they read, so when she passed out Squealer's first speech to the animals of Manor Farm, the kids knew just what to do. They had read the chapter containing the speech as homework, so this activity focused their attention for the period on this specific moment in the text. When the students completed their annotations, Liz opened the class to discussion, and they worked through their responses to and understanding of what the character was saying.

After this discussion, Liz distributed a list of terms associated with propaganda and shared definitions and examples of the terms with the class. To assess their initial understanding of the terms, she closed class by asking students to return to the left-hand column of the handout—the speech itself—and label examples of the devices of propaganda (see Figure 2.17). This work became the object of inquiry for three questions:

- Which students were demonstrating strong understanding of the novel, as indicated by their right-hand column annotations?

Figure 2.17: Student annotations on a passage from *Animal Farm*.

Text	Your Thoughts/Analysis
"Comrades," he said, "I trust that every animal here appreciates the sacrifice that Comrade Napoleon has made in taking this extra labour upon himself. Do not imagine, comrades, that leadership is a pleasure! On the contrary, it is a deep and heavy responsibility. No one believes more ~Identification~ firmly than Comrade Napoleon that all ~with Audience~ animals are equal. He would be only too happy to let you make your decisions for yourselves. But sometimes you might make the wrong decisions, comrades, ~Begging the Question~ and then where should we be? Suppose you had decided to follow Snowball, with his moonshine of windmills—Snowball, who, as we now ~Begging the question~ know, was no better than a criminal?" "He fought bravely at the Battle of the Cowshed," said somebody. "Bravery is not enough," said Squealer. ~Faulty cause and effect reasoning~ "Loyalty and obedience are more important. And as to the Battle of the ~Euphemism~ Cowshed, I believe the time will	Guilt in the animals for saying that leadership is very bad That Napoleon really cares for the animals and wants what is best for them Leaving the answer and consequences to the minds of the animals Saying that Snowball is a criminal by asking the question. He is saying that Bravery is not that important and is undermining Snowball's values and attitude. undermining Snowball's efforts

- Which students were demonstrating a strong understanding of the propaganda terms, as indicated by the left-hand column annotations?
- What persistent misconceptions were students demonstrating that she would need to address in the next day's instruction?

Liz used these questions to guide her analysis of student work, and she was able to sort students into higher-, middle-, and lower-level groups for the reading and analysis of a future speech. She also noticed that students were consistently mislabeling anything with a question mark in Squealer's speech as "begging the question." She made review and clarification of that concept the focus of the start of the next class session, after which she put students into mixed-performance groups to read, discuss, and analyze the next of Squealer's speeches. Although she couldn't meet with all of the groups at once, Liz was able to rely on the existing expertise of some of her students to provide support for those who were still developing an understanding.

After a few cycles of such assessment and instruction, Liz shared with students a real-world example of political propaganda, and students used the right-hand column to annotate both the propaganda devices and their impact on meaning, uniting the new content of the unit with the ongoing focus of her class—developing students who are capable of reading increasingly complex text with independence.

––––––––––

An important thread that joins these brief portraits of reading assessment in content area classrooms is that students were reading text they would have read anyway as part of the course. That's what makes a thoughtful, inquiry-based approach to adolescent reading assessment seem, in some ways, so unremarkable. These teachers aren't deploying sophisticated tools or inventories, though there are times that those are appropriate (see Chapter 5 for such a case). Instead, Faith and Liz are asking their students to respond to text in a way that will help these teachers investigate a question they already planned to respond to instructionally. Faith had a long-term, relatively low-intensity plan for response: individual student feedback and frequent opportunities to continue engaging in the act of reading and response. Liz's goals were more short term and high intensity: she changed instruction and student learning groups in immediate response to the work students produced and continued to monitor her three main questions until students were eventually ready to be assessed on independent performance.

Both approaches take heed of the dual notion of validity—construct and consequence. Students were reading real text and sharing their authentic, thoughtful responses; the teacher used their responses after careful analysis to uncover evidence manifested in their written and spoken responses, to guide instruction, and to provide appropriate support through full-class and more focused responses. These portraits, together with the more detailed scenarios earlier in the chapter, represent the foundation of the approach to adolescent literacy assessment that is further developed through examples in the next chapter.

Tools for Thought from Chapter 2

Building from the call for an inquiry approach to reading assessment in Chapter 1, this chapter offers a window into what it looks like to start asking questions and gathering evidence about students' reading abilities, habits, and attitudes. The assessment tools I describe offer three ways for you to get started with inquiry-based reading assessment with your own students:

- Sticky note annotations
- Student think-alouds and pre/postreading interview questions
- Pre/postreading questions and marginal annotations

The most appropriate tool for your context will depend on a number of factors, including the size of your class, the questions you have, and your level of comfort with this type of inquiry.

If the task seems daunting and the amount of information you might generate seems overwhelming, consider starting small. Ask a cooperative student to join you at lunch or before or after school to try the verbal interview. Give your students photocopies of the first few pages of the novel you're about to start in class and ask them to read independently while sharing their thoughts in the margins. Don't pressure yourself to start changing instruction immediately—though some cues might present themselves right away. The following chapters offer ideas on how to create a classroom structure and climate that not only allows for such assessment information to be taken up, but in fact requires it in order to function effectively.

Chapter Three

Formative Reading Assessment in Action

C hapter 2 explored the idea of approaching reading assessment as an act of inquiry and offered a few tools to help teachers encourage students to expose their thinking as readers—processes that by their cognitive and metacognitive nature are typically invisible. Central to that inquiry is posing well-formed inquiry questions to find evidence of the invisible "stuff" of reading comprehension, evidence purposefully sought to improve instruction and enhance student learning.

This chapter frames assessment as a more context-embedded process, whereby many of the same stances associated with teacher inquiry apply but within scenarios of acquisition of content knowledge and skills. Specifically, the portraits of Chris Belt's ninth-grade English class, with a focus on learning to summarize, and Will Aldridge's Ancient Civilizations course, with a focus on interpreting and applying Confucian analects, demonstrate how classroom-based formative assessment fuels the stages of the gradual release of responsibility (GRR) model (Fisher & Frey, 2008a; Frey, Fisher, & Everlove, 2009; Fisher & Frey, 2010).

Based on a model for supporting reading comprehension in younger learners (Pearson & Gallagher, 1983), the GRR model provides a framework for organizing instructional time and routines, purposefully moving from teacher responsibility, typically through modeling or thinking aloud, to student responsibility, eventually through independent practice. The GRR model has gained traction in my district because it provides a means for enacting a "curriculum committed to independent learning . . . built on the premise that inquiry, rather than mere transmission of knowledge, is the basis of teaching and learning" (SARW, p. 2). Consequently, as teachers in our building have begun framing instruction around the model in various content area classrooms, we've discovered that GRR *requires* us to assess students informally to know how to proceed with the next instructional step. Teaching with the GRR model feels very different from our typical approach because it takes gaps in and variations of student development as a given, not something to be afraid of or surprised by. Assessing "for the gradebook" therefore naturally takes a backseat to assessing to improve teaching and learning.

The model, which is deceptively straightforward and seemingly linear at first blush, involves four components:

- *Focus lessons:* Teacher responsibility is high because he or she sets the purpose for instruction and provides a model for thinking through the new content, text, or problem.

- *Guided instruction:* As we've taken it up at our school, guided instruction often involves creating temporary homogeneous groups (based on the results of purposeful assessment) that allow for focused questioning and in-the-moment checking for understanding to guide students in new learning.

- *Group work:* Typically more heterogeneous (think splitting apart and re-distributing the groups from guided instruction), teacher involvement here becomes a bit more supervisory as students work together to consolidate new learning while producing individual, assessable products.

- *Independent tasks:* Teacher involvement is minimal as students work on their own to demonstrate their developing competence. As we implement GRR at our school, this is the only step at which students are assessed summatively. All other assessment information is used only to guide the next steps in the cycle.

Because GRR is a framework or model for instruction, it appears simpler on paper than it ever is in actual implementation. That said, the two iterations of GRR I describe in this chapter are relatively straightforward, both because that's how the implementations really happened and because the clarity of implementation will highlight the central role that formative assessment plays in helping teachers know how to move from one step to another.

All of the assessment tools you'll read about in this chapter are teacher created and specific to the classroom context in which they were used. We know that some publishers of textbooks and other materials, eager to cash in on the formative assessment craze but wholly unable to deliver the high degree of professional responsiveness that formative assessment actually requires, advertise formative assessment as a feature of their products. Similarly, as the Common Core State Standards assessment machine gears up for implementation in 2014, there is talk of "through-course" assessments that are framed as formative—providing information to teachers and students on the path toward the "real test" at the end of the year. Suffice it to say that neither of these corruptions of formative assessment is what the teachers discussed in this chapter are doing. Rather, you'll find them using assessment as inquiry as they develop clear instructional goals and adjust the learning environment toward increased proficiency in response to how students perform in the stages of GRR.

Standing in Mr. Belt's Shoes: Teaching and Learning Summarization in the Context of *To Kill a Mockingbird*

Chris Belt teaches honors ninth-grade English. Despite the honors designation, Chris and the other teachers of the course know that the range of student ability in their classrooms is far from narrow. Interested in getting to know their students better as thinkers and readers, Chris and his course-alike colleagues developed a preassessment that they use at the beginning of the year to start noting the areas in which students succeed and struggle.

Because the course focuses on the literary concept of conflict in the first semester, they chose a short, high-interest online news article about three white men (two of whom were teens, one of whom was older and had ties to a white supremacist group) charged with attacking an older African American man, James Privott, while he was out fishing with his wife, Ethel (see the 2009 article, "Adult, Two

At the beginning of the year, Chris and his colleagues sought a greater understanding of the very broad question "How well do my students read?" They used the aspects of summary, inference, and author's purpose, not to oversimplify the act of reading into three neat categories but rather to provide focus and manageability to the assessment. If you've selected text that you might use to begin inquiry into your students' ability to read and respond to it, read the text carefully to determine what cognitive work is required of *you* as you read it. If you annotate text as you read, you'll get a sense of the kinds of questions you might ask to assess your students' comprehension. As a bonus, these annotations might serve as the basis for a think-aloud if you were to use the text to model comprehension.

Teens Charged with Beating Elderly Black Man," at http://articles.cnn
.com/2009-08-20/justice/maryland.racial.attack_1_calvin-lockner-police-beating?
_s=PM:CRIME). From this text, the teachers developed a set of short open
response questions that target students' ability to

- Make generalizations and draw conclusions ("Why would someone want the
  nickname 'Hitler'?" and "How will Ethel Privott's behavior change after the
  incident?")
- Articulate the author's purpose for making various choices ("Why does the
  author of the article include the detail that there was no evidence to link the
  teens with the white supremacist group?" and "Why did the author of the
  article include Ethel's statements so often?")
- Detect main ideas and summarize ("Summarize the central conflict.")

On the day Chris gave the preassessment to his first-hour ninth graders, he
began by telling them they would be reading and responding to some questions but
that the work would not be for a grade; instead, it would give him valuable information about what they can do and how they think. "Take your time; there's no
rush and no pressure," Chris assured the class as he distributed the assessment materials. Even so, one student blurted out, "Is this an *extended response*? I'm not very
good at writing those." This student's question refers to the term describing part
of our state's eighth-grade reading assessment and suggests his close association of
standardized testing with the word *assessment*, as well as a negative association with
both. I mention this exchange to stress that everyone in the classroom brings an
assessment history with him or her (see Chapter 1). Although we too infrequently
seek to uncover them or try to address them, those histories, like the dimensions of
reading discussed in Chapter 1, are always at play as students take a test or perform
any assessment.

Students read and wrote for about twenty-five minutes, a small investment of
time for the information the assessment gave Chris—particularly since the content
of the article also allowed the class to immediately begin discussing the continued
presence of racial prejudice and conflict in our society, good preparation for the
full-class reading of Harper Lee's *To Kill a Mockingbird*. Chris's team of course-
alike teachers had designed a concise rubric (see Figure 3.1) that allows him to read
student responses, make descriptive or observational notes on each student's paper,
and assign a numerical score to add a bit of clarity to the written notes. We found
that for these purposes, the precise number we agreed to assign to a student's
response wasn't quite as important as the conversations we had about what the
student was saying and the thinking he or she revealed. These numbers, after all,
were not going to become part of the student's grade; this assessment was purely
formative and the numerical data were descriptive rather than evaluative.

Figure 3.1: This preassessment rubric allowed Chris to assign a numerical level of performance to the students' responses to questions designed to assess the skills of summarizing main ideas, making generalizations and drawing conclusions, and stating the author's purpose.

	Main ideas/Summary
4	The student summarizes adeptly with most of the important ideas clearly expressed and supported with accurate details and facts.
3	The student summarizes adequately with a main idea expressed and supported with some accurate details and facts.
2	The student partially summarizes and may misinterpret the main idea or fail to express it clearly; includes a few details and facts but may also offer up some unimportant information.
1	The student includes a few facts, which may or may not be important information, but does not express a main idea.

	Generalizations and conclusions
4	The student consistently draws reasonable and accurate conclusions using evidence from the text and general prior knowledge.
3	The student shows some evidence of the ability to draw reasonable and accurate conclusions using evidence from the text or from general prior knowledge.
2	The student shows the ability to draw simple conclusions from relatively straightforward evidence from the text, but may be unable to do so from general prior knowledge.
1	The student shows little ability to draw conclusions from the text.

	Author's purpose
4	Given a particular rhetorical strategy, the student can identify, evaluate, or infer the intent of the author.
3	Given a particular rhetorical strategy, the student can identify but not consistently evaluate or infer the intent of the author.
2	Given a particular rhetorical strategy, the student can identify but can neither evaluate nor infer the intent of the author.
1	Given a particular rhetorical strategy, the student cannot identify, evaluate, or infer the intent of the author.

Student sample responses to the preassessment demonstrated a sense of the range within the class. For example, Bailey (see Figure 3.2) demonstrates a solid understanding of the article, articulating a fairly sophisticated summary of the text and showing a sense of the appropriate balance between main ideas and details in an effective summary. Still, Chris scored Bailey as a 3 on all elements of the rubric because of the unevenness of her responses relating to generalizations and author's purpose and the overreliance on details at the expense of main idea in the summary.

Figure 3.2: Bailey's preassessment.

Answer the following questions in complete sentences.

1. Why would someone want the nickname Hitler?

   Lockner was obviosly a racist person, as was Hitler.

2. Why does the author of the article include the detail that there was no evidence to link the teens with a white supremacist group?

   The author said that there was no evidence of the teens being involved in a white group, because that may mean that the teens weren't as racist / and Lockmer was the prime attacker.

3. How will Ethel Privott's behavior change after the incident?

   Ethel will most likely be very careful and never be out by herself.

4. Why did the author of the article include Ethel's statements so often?

   Ethel knew what went on normally arround the area her husband was attacked. It normally had a lot of old folks around to fish.

5. Summarize the central conflict.

   3 white men (2 teens, 1 adult) attacked a black 76 year old James Privott who suffered severe head injuries in the attack. The suspects robbed him and left. The adult (Calvin Lockman) was involved in a white supremist group. Police "say" it had a racial connection.

Rich, on the other hand, demonstrates understanding, but with less sophistication and less attention to the elements of an effective summary (see Figure 3.3). Chris scored Rich as a 1.5 on all the elements of the rubric because his responses to questions about generalizations and author's purpose revealed only the beginnings of proficiency. Rich's summary focuses on a high-level main idea but isn't terribly accurate as he falls prey to the allure of the global term *white supremacist* rather than contextualizing its specific function in the article.

As Chris and I read through students' widely ranging responses to the preassessment, we saw that almost all of them, including Bailey and Rich, would benefit from instruction on summarizing, particularly in separating detailed retelling from

Figure 3.3: Rich's preassessment.

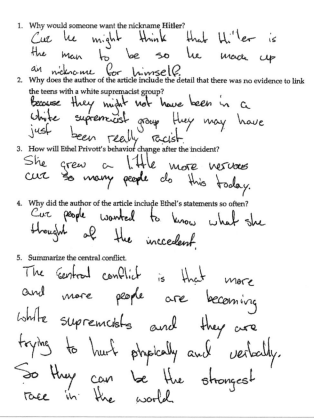

Answer the following questions in complete sentences.

1. Why would someone want the nickname **Hitler**?

   Cuz he might think that Hitler is the man to be so he made up an nickname for himself.

2. Why does the author of the article include the detail that there was no evidence to link the teens with a white supremacist group?

   Because they might not have been in a white supremacist group they may have just been really racist.

3. How will Ethel Privott's behavior change after the incident?

   She grew a little more nervous cuz so many people do this today.

4. Why did the author of the article include Ethel's statements so often?

   Cuz people wanted to know what she thought of the inccedent.

5. Summarize the central conflict.

   The central conflict is that more and more people are becoming white supremcists and they are trying to hurt physically and verbally. So they can be the strongest race in the world

focused summary. But Chris's students needed more than summary know-how; based on their preassessment performance, they needed differentiated learning experiences that gave them a chance to interact with text that would continue to prepare them for reading *To Kill a Mockingbird* and offer them an appropriate level of challenge.

Therefore, we decided to use text complexity as the means to differentiate guided instruction for this instructional step. Chris used the preassessment information to begin putting students into four levels of groups, ranging from clusters of students who showed the most proficiency with language, interpretation, and summary to those who showed they needed the most support. In the company of peers of similar ability, a student such as Bailey could be given a more challenging text to begin applying the standards for effective summary; Rich could probably

Though it comes from the field of writing studies, Peter Elbow's (1993) essay "Ranking, Evaluating, and Liking: Sorting Out Three Forms of Judgment" informs much of the thinking described in this section. Elbow writes, "Assessment is a large and technical area and I'm not a professional. But my main premise or subtext in this essay is that we nonprofessionals can and should work on it because professionals have not reached definitive conclusions about the problem of how to assess writing (or anything else, I'd say). Also, decisions about assessment are often made by people even less professional than we, namely legislators" (p. 187). More to the point, Elbow goes on to theorize the differences between ranking (holistic grading, with stakes attached), evaluating (feature-based analysis, sometimes with stakes attached and sometimes not), and *liking* the work students produce (which he describes as both "represent[ing] the worst kind of subjectivity, the merest accident of personal taste" and being "perhaps the most important evaluative response for writers and teachers to think about" (p. 199). I consider this a challenging and foundational essay for thinking through what it means to respond to student work. When you start looking at student work from an inquiry perspective, try to be deliberate about your purpose: Are you ranking students into groups? Evaluating against criteria, as if to assign standards-based grades? Reading to develop a deeper understanding of your kids as readers and learners? While not mutually exclusive, these stances are definitely different.

use something a little less complex so that he could focus more on the elements of summary than on the challenge of reading the text.

Because we wanted to keep this assessment and instruction cycle as authentic as possible, we looked for short texts that would continue to build students' prior knowledge while they practiced summarizing. By luck, we discovered that an edition of *To Kill a Mockingbird* in our school bookroom included a selection of brief related readings, which served our purpose well (see Figure 3.4).

With the content and assessment information in place to begin the instructional cycle, Chris prepared a focus lesson (see Figure 3.5) for the whole class on

Figure 3.4: Texts Chris used to generate background knowledge on *To Kill a Mockingbird* while differentiating students' reading and summarizing experiences.

Excerpt from *Growing Up in the Great Depression* by Richard Wormser	This reading was the basis of Chris's focus lesson and think-aloud, a nonfiction text that would help students understand the economic conditions in Maycomb during the time of the novel.
• "The Right Thing to Do at the Time" by George Garrett • "You Wouldn't Understand" by José Emilio Pacheco • "The Hidden Songs of a Secret Soul" by Bob Greene	Chris used the text complexity rubric from the ACT, with a focus on the elements of relationships, richness, structure, style, vocabulary, and purpose (see http://www.act.org/research/policymakers/pdf/reading_summary.pdf), to rank these texts—each of which explores a theme, issue, or character type that relates to those of *To Kill a Mockingbird*—from least to most complex in order to provide his students with different levels of challenge. The rubric is an imperfect but useful means for thinking about text complexity beyond syllable count, word frequency, and sentence length—the traditional components in determining how challenging a text is to read.

Figure 3.5: Chris's plan for the focus lesson.

Purpose of Summary
- Essential to development as thinkers and writers
- Helps to learn about and remember a text

Important Processes
- Delete minor or redundant details
- Combine similar details into categories
- Select main idea sentences when they're in the text; create them when necessary

Steps to Summarizing
- Recognize text structure
  - Examples: Narrative, exposition, fiction, nonfiction, cause–effect, problem–solution, compare–contrast, chronology
  - Text structure affects the placement of a main idea and the form in which it may appear
  - Text structures have certain words that can cue the type of structure
- Generalize from details
  - Details build up to—or generate from—a main idea
- Identify the main ideas

Summary no-no's/Misconceptions
- Copy-delete: Copying the text word for word and deleting a few words
- A simple sequential retelling of the text

—Adapted from Dean (2011)

Text of full-class reading in the left column, Chris's think-aloud in the right.

In 1930 America went bust. A great economic depression settled over the country like a plague, afflicting the rich and the poor, men, women, and children, black and white, foreign- and native-born, workers and farmers. Millions of people lost their jobs, their businesses, their farms, their homes, their savings, and their self respect.	*Okay, so I see a lot of details in this paragraph about who the Depression affected. In order to summarize, I need to generalize them by saying, "The depression affected people from all walks of life, economically and emotionally."*
It all seemed to happen suddenly. For ten years the country seemed to be on a spending spree. In 1920, 7.5 million automobiles had been purchased. By 1929, there were 26.5 million. The sales of goods rose from $4.9 billion in 1920 to $7.06 billion in 1929. Industry was booming. From 1925 to 1929, the number of factories increased from 183,877 to 206,663. More high school students were graduating than ever before (from 16 percent in 1920 to 28 percent in 1930). . . .	*This paragraph is heavy on details too, and I notice it's structured by comparison from early in the decade to late. I'm thinking I just need to remember that lots of important signs made it seem like things were much better at the end of the '20s than at the beginning.*
The index of America's prosperity was Wall Street and the stock market. From the end of World War I in 1919, stock prices kept rising. In 1924, the average price of the twenty-five leading industrial stocks in America was $120 a share. By 1929, the same stocks were worth $542. Many people believed they had found a money machine that could not fail. Everybody knew somebody—or so they said—who had bought a stock at $10 one day and sold it for $20 the next.	*So the stock market is something I really associate with the Great Depression. It looks like the author is giving the stock market as another example of something that had really inflated in the ten years before the crash.*

the features of an effective summary, sharing with students the purposes of summarizing, such as its usefulness in helping readers learn and remember more about what we read (Deborah Dean's book *What Works in Writing Instruction: Research and Practices* [2011] was invaluable in helping us think through this focus lesson). Chris was careful to include the element of purpose in his focus lesson because informal conversations with his students revealed that students had little understanding of *why* they were asked to summarize so often in school-based assignments. The focus lesson included a strong emphasis on the importance of a synthesized main idea statement and an attempt to move beyond a sequential retelling, both of which had revealed themselves as problems in the preassessment.

Chris read aloud the Wormser text on the Great Depression (see the left-hand column in Figure 3.5), thinking through—again aloud—what he saw as important ideas and significant details (see the right-hand column), which naturally shifted as the text went on to describe more and more causes of the Depression. He then wrote a brief paragraph on the overhead that summarized the text, using the academic language of *main idea*, *text structure*, and *significant details* as he wrote to emphasize some of the key concepts associated with summarizing. At the end of the period, Chris asked students to write briefly about some of the things they learned about summarizing from watching him go through the process.

The difference between assessment for a one-time instructional adjustment and ongoing, content-embedded formative assessment will become obvious as Chris and his students progress through the GRR framework. Assessment information guides Chris's instructional decisions as he moves from one step in the cycle to another; more important, in-the-moment assessment of student learning helps him know what to do *within* the class period as well. As you continue to read, consider how this example of differentiated instruction might be similar to or different from ways you've encountered it in your practice or in professional development around the topic.

After reading the students' end-of-class writings, Chris was ready to prepare the next phase of learning, guided instruction using leveled texts as the point of differentiation. He began the next class session by putting on the overhead some of the end-of-class student-generated responses that explained their new understanding of summarizing:

- The need to generalize details by creating categories
- The need to delete some details that seem unimportant
- The difference between summary and retelling
- The purpose of summary as a learning tool

Chris then explained that students would be reading a short story in class and applying what he'd taught about summary. Using the leveled groupings suggested by the preassessment information, coupled with his general knowledge of his students, Chris announced the student groupings and distributed the three leveled texts as students jotted down the names of their partners for the collaborative portion of the lesson. Students read silently and then formed their groups to begin discussing their stories and how they might try to capture them most effectively through summary.

Because of the temporary ability-level grouping underlying this activity, Chris knew that the first groups he would visit to assess informally and provide guidance were the ones who read the least complex text, "The Right Thing to Do at the Time." The power of summary as a learning tool became clear to students as Chris asked these groups initial prompting questions such as "What seems most important?" or "How might you start your summary?" Using the framework set forth in Fisher and Frey (2010), Chris used students' answers to such basic questions to facilitate three different types of responses as he moved among the groups:

- *Prompting:* When students seemed stuck on definitions of aspects of summary or steps in the process of summarizing, Chris provided support by reminding them of the content of the previous day's focus lesson. And when students shared with Chris lists of content they might use in a summary, he prompted them to differentiate between content that was more detail oriented and that which was more "big idea" oriented.

- *Cueing:* Chris noticed that one group was beginning its summary with the first event of the story, so he cued them to consider whether there might be a better way to begin—to avoid a retelling such as those he saw in the preassessment.

- *Explaining and modeling:* When students seemed stuck, offering responses that revealed significant misunderstanding or frustration with the task, Chris sat down with the group to read a paragraph or two aloud with them and think aloud about what seemed important and what didn't, using the processes and academic language from the previous day's focus lesson.

This high-intensity, in-the-moment assessment and response was a new stance that Chris was working to develop. When we met to examine student work and reflect on how the lesson went, Chris rightly pointed out how much deep knowledge of the subject matter this type of instruction requires. In a classroom differentiated based on students' ability to handle different levels of text complexity, students are reading multiple texts at the same time, and Chris had to be prepared to leap from one story to another from moment to moment as he circulated among the groups, providing guidance and support.

This differentiated structure differs from the typical high school instructional model that puts a single text at the center of instruction, reducing the burden on the teacher but keeping some students from accessing the text and potentially not challenging others. Indeed, responding to what we learn from assessment does not lessen the workload for anyone involved, but it gives more students a better chance of getting the appropriate work for them to develop the skills and understandings we want them to have.

As discussed, one instructional response to assessment data is to offer students texts of varying complexity, which allows for a closer match to students' level of development than any single text could. Consider a place in an existing unit from your own curriculum where such differentiation might be possible. Before beginning a novel or other major work, look online for a range of nonfiction articles that offer background knowledge on that text or topic. Rank them in order of complexity, matching them to students for reading and discussion in groups. If varying the text level isn't possible, consider different levels of scaffolding for groups of varying ability. One group might get a set of focused questions and a glossary; a second might receive just the glossary; a third might receive no scaffolding.

That said, Chris was still somewhat disappointed when he looked at student summaries and found that, while they often chose relevant details to include, for the most part they didn't present a thoughtful main idea statement. Bailey's summary (Figure 3.6), for example, selects just the right details about the character Lenny, who is a lot like Boo Radley in his hesitant desire to reach out to a world of people he knows he's different from, but the details don't constitute a main idea statement. Similarly, Rich's work (Figure 3.7) contains the beginnings of a summary but doesn't synthesize the details he's selected into a main idea statement about the courage it takes to stand up to racism that is deeply entrenched in a community. As Chris drafted supportive written feedback that pointed out students' success in noticing what was important to include but also prompted them to think about how those details work together to suggest a bigger, perhaps unstated, main idea, we reminded ourselves that careful assessment does *eventually* lead to success for a higher number of students, but that the learning process is still a process. Assessment doesn't guarantee quick success, but when done well, it increases the likelihood of an instructional response that promotes growth.

"Most standardized tests compare students to one another, while teachers' comments can be specific and individualized, providing a clear picture of each student's special strengths and weaknesses" (SARW, p. 15). Chris used three guiding questions (Stiggins et al., qtd. in Overlie, 2009) and three specific practices (Brookhart, 2008) to frame the feedback he offered students on their summaries:

Questions	Implied Feedback Practice
Where am I going?	Remind student of what the successful completion of the reading task will look like.
Where am I now?	Describe specific aspects of the student work in relation to the goal.
How can I close the gap?	Engage the student in self-reflection by asking questions or offering multiple strategies that he or she might use to improve this work or to do better the next time.

Figure 3.6: Bailey's summary.

<u>The Hidden Songs of a Secret Soul</u>
Summary

Lenny was a quiet personal man that worked full time at a soda bottling plant. Other "full-timers" teased him, but he liked it better when he was left alone. The part-time College students befriended Lenny and Lenny told them about the poems that he wrote. Although they were beautiful, Lenny refused the college student permission to tell anyone about them.

Figure 3.7: Rich's summary.

The right thing to do at the right time.

10/22/10

This story was a man going to Tallehassee for a traffic ticket. And to prove that kissimmee is a bad town to go to. Because a cop broke his tailight because he didn't like the lawyer. He also didn't like him because he was fighting the kkk.

As students began reading *To Kill a Mockingbird*, Chris continued to develop instruction that responded to the strengths and weaknesses students revealed through formative assessment, including an activity that allowed him to flip the teacher and student roles. Chris wrote three possible summaries of the first few chapters of the novel and students became the assessors, listing the strengths and weaknesses of the summaries and offering a score based on a four-point rubric describing the features of effective summary (see Figure 3.8).

Figure 3.8: Sample summaries to allow students to practice assessment themselves.

Summary #2

The point of these first four chapters is to introduce us to the Deep South. It strives to acquaint us with the characters and the plot. We meet Scout and Jem, the narration being told from Scout's point of view. She dictates a brief history of Maycomb and then shows us the town itself. We learn about the Radley's and then Dill, the boy who purportedly started it all. Scout goes to school (showing us the inadequacy of the teacher) and saves Walter Cunningham from disgrace. All through these chapters, the narrator doesn't spare us an emotion, or a memory from a long forgotten place. We read the story through Scout's eyes, the naiveté of a young southern girl delighted with the prospect of a mystery.

Strengths:	Weaknesses:
Goes deeper than just stating the details · Recognizes text structure · Main idea statement · The reader seems very involved with the text	Not many details
Score: 4	

Summary #3

So far in the story, it is mostly describing the characters and plot of the book. So far it showed the kids going to school and their problems. Such as Scout experienced her first day of school with a teacher who partially disliked her.

Strengths:	Weaknesses:
· Generalizes details	· No main idea · Tells what the story involves not what the story is about · Deleted too many details · No recognition of text structure
Score: 2	

This kind of instruction prepared students for the next phase of the GRR cycle, the collaborative learning phase, in which Chris arranged students in mixed-ability groups and gave each group the same text: a rather lengthy, detail-filled article on the Scottsboro boys that provides a thematic parallel to the injustice Tom Robinson faces in *To Kill a Mockingbird*. In a process that looked similar to the like-ability groupings from earlier in the cycle, but with Chris intervening less as students depended more on one another and the skills they were developing, students produced summaries such as the ones depicted in Figures 3.9 and 3.10. There is still a noticeable difference in sophistication between the summaries of Bailey and Rich:

- Bailey includes the sentence "The case was incredibly unjust and the young men's lives were hurt terribly by the events," which reveals the element of synthesis that Chris had been emphasizing.

- Rich's main idea statement remains rather topical: "This article is about nine men who were falsely accused of raping two white women on a train."

Both summaries are competent performances of the task. More important, both are better written and reveal more sophistication and insight than those Bailey and Rich composed earlier in the unit.

The independent task in Chris Belt's English class, summarizing a written piece to synthesize the main idea and offer some key details, was ongoing as students studied *To Kill a Mockingbird* (see Figures 3.11 and 3.12 for a look at how Bailey and Rich continued to reveal their understanding of the novel through summaries). Chris didn't attempt a culminating assessment, because development of

Figure 3.9: Bailey's summary.

Spring, 1931, 9 black young men were accused falsely of raping two white women who were on a train with the boys. Several white men had called the police and falsely accused the boys. They were sentenced to death or life imprisonment until the ILD got involved. There were many more trials and every time the young men were unjustly sentenced until, finally, the 4 boys got their charges dropped and the other 5 were sentenced to a long time in prison. The case was incredibly unjust and the young men's lives were hurt terribly by the events.

Figure 3.10: Rich's summary.

Summary

10-26-10

This article is about a nine men who were falsely accused of raping two white women on a train. They all had trials in the Alabama Court System and they were all found guilty by all-white juries. They faced lengthy terms in jail. But then all of them were dropped of there charges and went to the Supreme Court for their trials. But the jery came back guilty and the death penalty. But Judge James Horton overruled them and the trial was heard again. Four of them were found guilty and four were let go. The last one was shot in the head.

summarization is an ongoing process, particularly as text becomes more challenging. In this regard, the following portrait of ongoing assessment in a gradual release of responsibility instructional cycle in Will Aldridge's semester-long Ancient Civilizations class differs significantly from Chris's class: it *begins* with the creation of the culminating performance task and then backward maps learning and assessment activities to prepare students for that task.

Figure 3.11: Bailey's independent summary (with planning).

Summary Organizer:

Details:

- Heak Tate, the Sheriff, brings the news that the cruel Bob Ewell was dead
  - Bob's last act was to attack Atticus' children as a way to get revenge.
- Atticus trys to discipline his children even if it means incriminating Jem
  - Heck Tate and Atticus argue about how Bob died.
  - Atticus thought that Jem killed Bob, in defence of scout and himself
  - Heck realizes that Bob killed himself
- Scout is begining to understand some of the cruelty of life
- Scout leads Boo home
  - Boo's innocence shows how he is child-like. and does ...
  - Scout is growing up
  - She has empathy for Boo and realizes how he has cared for Jem, Dill, and herself

Main Idea Statement: In sthe chapters 29 through 31, Heck Tate sums up to the Finches how Bob Ewell attacked Jem and Scout and ended up, killing himself. It also is an importat point in Scout begining to grow into an Adult.

In chapters 29 through 31, Heck Tate sums up how Bob Ewell attacked Atticus' children and then killed himself to the Finch family. It is also an important point in scout stepping towards adulthood. Hech explains that Bob Ewell was drunk and just plain mean and as his last act he tried to get revenge on Atticus by attacking his children. Atticus thinks that, in an effort to defend his sister and himself, Jem killed Bob Ewell, but Heck Tate argued that Jem couldn't possibly have killed Bob. He says that Bob actually killed himself. Boo Radly had carried Jem home and was listening quietly for a while until it was time to leave and he asked Scout to lead him home showing Boo's innocence as a child-like adult. After Scout leads him to his house she realizes how Boo has cared for Jem, Dill, and herself. This also shows how much Scout has grown up over the course of the past chapters.

Figure 3.12: Rich's independent summary plan.

Summary Organizer:

Details:

- Bob Ewell supposedly fell on his knife.
- Bob Ewell tried to kill Jem and Scout on the way home from the Halloween Pageant.

Main Idea Statement:

Bob Ewell Died

Developing Content Area Understanding through Reading and Assessment

As part of their study of ancient China, Will and his ninth-grade students were going to be learning about the historical figure of Confucius, using the primary source of the Confucian analects to better understand the era and its dominant persona and philosophy. Will and I began our collaboration by discussing together two questions that would frame the instructional process:

- What's challenging about reading and interpreting Confucian analects?
- How do you define a successful reading and interpretation of Confucian analects?

By this point, the value of good questions to successful inquiry-based assessment should be clear, but notice that these specific questions are of a slightly different nature from those that prompted other teaching and learning cycles discussed in this book. These are "teacher-facing" questions—questions about the nature of the content under study, not about the students' current level of performance and not for the students to answer (although it might be useful to share them with students at appropriate moments during instruction). These are not the questions that inquiry-based assessments seek to answer; rather, they're the questions that help set a teaching context and a vision for what successful achievement of the reading and interpretation task might look like. In Chris Belt's classroom, the theory of successful summarization pulled from Deborah Dean's (2011) book, and embedded in his focus lesson described in Figure 3.5, served a purpose similar to this conversation between Will and me.

Will is an extremely thoughtful teacher who has the benefit of working with equally thoughtful colleagues on his course-alike team, so he had ready answers to these questions. He noted that in the past, students had misperceived the brevity of the analects for simplicity and had trouble understanding that they represent a whole persona and cultural philosophy. The vast differences between modern American life and that of ancient China also elicit a range of confounding student prior knowledge, such as conflicting views on the role and value of the individual and gender equality. (I take up the topic of assessing prior knowledge as a tool for aiding comprehension in the next chapter.) Add challenging vocabulary to the mix, and the significance of the task Will faced was clear.

Even clearer, however, was Will's sense of what a successful interpretation of a Confucian analect involved, a specific description of success tied to an overarching goal for the class. He wanted students to be able to explain what an analect meant in the context of the Chinese society in which it was created while also applying its message to a modern American situation or problem. We used this goal to create a performance task modeled on the guidelines of Wiggins and McTighe (2005), in which students are given the opportunity to reveal their understandings through an authentic, real-world problem with no clear solution but with clear roles for writer and audience. This prompt, Figure 3.13, became the goal toward which Will's instruction was aimed.

Knowing that success with this task was at this point well beyond the reach of his students, Will prepared a brief background lecture on Confucius and his times and then, as a preassessment of student ability, asked students to interpret and paraphrase four analects:

1. The Master said, "It is a rare thing for someone who has a sense of filial and fraternal responsibility to have a taste for defying authority. And it is unheard of for those who have no taste for defying authority to be keen on initiating rebellion. Exemplary persons concentrate their efforts on the root, for the root having taken hold, the way will grow therefrom. As for filial and fraternal responsibility, it is, I suspect the root of authoritative conduct."

2. The Master said, "Lead the people with administrative injunctions and keep them orderly with penal law, and they will avoid punishments but will be without a sense of shame. Lead them with excellence and keep them orderly through observing ritual propriety and they will develop a sense of shame, and moreover, will order themselves."

3. The Master said, "Exemplary persons understand what is appropriate; petty persons understand what is of personal advantage."

4. The Master said, "Exemplary persons make demands on themselves, while petty persons make demands on others."

An inquiry approach to reading assessment requires flexibility—part of the reason why packaged approaches to formative assessment don't make much sense. I find it useful to have a likely instructional response (e.g., temporarily grouping students by demonstrated proficiency at a given task) in mind when approaching a classroom set of preassessments. If the student work doesn't support your initial planned response, however, you need to determine a different, appropriate response to maintain the validity of the assessment. See the ideas connected to the record-keeping chart in Figure 2.7 for more discussion.

When we met to review the work students produced in response to this preassessment (Figures 3.14–3.16), our goal was to sort students into like-ability groups for guided instruction that used analects of varying difficulty as the mode of differentiation. While the examples of student work suggest the range of student ability at the time of preassessment, Will found that a significantly large portion of the class fell in the "indiscernible middle." We could identify a few students who had some exceptional strength at the task already, but most lacked the background in vocabulary and Confucian thinking—and the

---

Figure 3.13: Performance task to assess students' ability to comprehend and apply Confucian analects.

You are an advisor to an American politician who is considering a run for the presidency in 2012. The politician has asked you to review influential thinking on government from different cultural and historical figures, and you found this collection of Confucian analects particularly interesting.

Your task is to choose some of the most important or interesting ideas from the analects and write a memo to your candidate explaining what you've learned and how you feel it would be useful advice for a contemporary American national leader.

- First, think through each analect carefully and write a brief paraphrase in the appropriate box on the sheet provided. **Remember to paraphrase the analects from a Confucian perspective;** don't let your modern American point of view influence the ideas the analects express.

- Circle any words you don't know and ask for clarification of their meanings.

- Try to refer to all or parts of all four of the analects in your memo, making note of advice that you think applies to contemporary America. Include references to specific real-world problems and issues to show how the advice is relevant or useful.

- If possible, include discussion of the Five Relationships and/or the Way* to demonstrate your understanding of the analects.

---

*The Five Relationships refer to specific duties given to the participants of the relationships involving ruler and ruled, father and son, husband and wife, elder to younger sibling, and friend to friend; the Way refers to the absolute moral and philosophical path on which the faithful move.

---

confidence to try to paraphrase something quite challenging—and thus we had to alter our original plan.

Still, the preassessment was quite useful because it provided a baseline level of performance for each student for comparison at the end of the unit, and it revealed some student misconceptions that Will could address in the think-alouds through the focus lesson with which he began each class period on Confucius. For example, students either ignored or misinterpreted the focus on shame in the second analect, evidence Will interpreted as a cultural mismatch that he would have to address directly to help them understand both the analect itself and the larger worldview it embodies. In a highly routine-driven plan for this unit (which, coming toward the end of the semester, had to be taught rather compactly), Will ended each lesson with students reading and responding to an analect, which allowed him to follow this pattern:

Focus lesson: Interpret a selected analect by thinking aloud, responding to perceived needs of students from preassessment/earlier response, reminding students of the unit's essential question: "To what extent did Confucius impact social order?"

Content lesson: Lecture/discussion or reading on Confucian society, the Five
                 Relationships, the Way.
Wrap up: Students interpret (through discussion or in writing) an analect
          related to the day's content as an ungraded check for under-
          standing.

The compact nature of this unit didn't allow Will to provide significant written
feedback on each student's interpretation, but with the structure of the focus lesson
in place, he could note the kinds of challenges students were facing and make those
the focus of his feedback. As he continued to see students struggle with challenging vocabulary, for example, he focused a think-aloud on strategies for responding
to unfamiliar words, ranging from using context clues to consulting a dictionary
or other resource when appropriate. When students continued to misapply their
background knowledge and view of the world, he demonstrated his process for
thinking through the confusion that comes with approaching life from a stance
that is potentially at odds with what seems so natural and familiar to the adolescent
learners in his classroom.

After students had been exposed to sufficient background knowledge and had
more experience reading and responding to analects, Will used the preassessment
information and any new insights he'd gained through reading their daily responses to organize students heterogeneously for some purposeful group work. Given
the task of interpreting an analect and applying it to a real-world modern problem,

Figure 3.14: Maria's response to the preassessment.

1. I have no idea.

2. If you lead people the right way you'll get good things in advance?

3. Some people know whats more important while others dont?

4. Some people are more selfish than others.

Figure 3.15: Elizabeth's response to the preassessment.

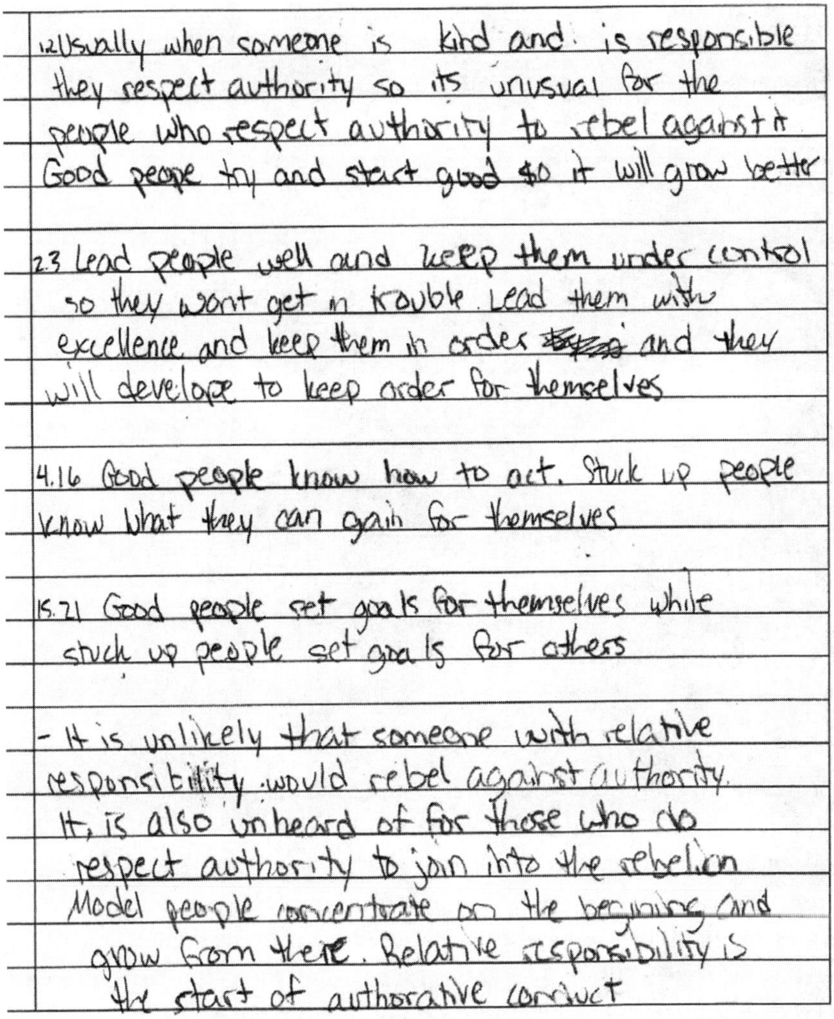

> 12Usually when someone is kind and is responsible they respect authority so its unusual for the people who respect authority to rebel against it. Good people try and start good so it will grow better
>
> 23 Lead people well and keep them under control so they wont get in trouble. Lead them with excellence and keep them in order and they will develope to keep order for themselves
>
> 4.16 Good people know how to act. Stuck up people know what they can gain for themselves
>
> 15.21 Good people set goals for themselves while stuck up people set goals for others
>
> - It is unlikely that someone with relative responsibility would rebel against authority. It is also unheard of for those who do respect authority to join into the rebelion. Model people concentrate on the begining and grow from there. Relative responsibility is the start of authorative conduct

groups received a few analects and at first could only *talk* about their responses with one another, though they would each submit a written response at the end of the period. To keep the groups from functioning as independent workers sharing only a table—and to keep stronger students in the group from providing *the* response that everyone else writes down—Will withheld the note card on which students needed to compose their responses until he had met with each group

Figure 3.16: Derron's response to the preassessment.

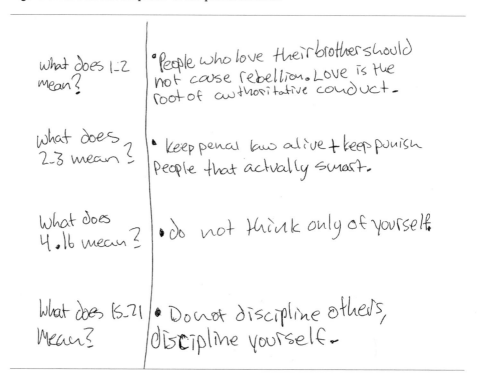

what does 1-2 mean?

• People who love their brother should not cause rebellion. Love is the root of authoritative conduct.

what does 2-3 mean?

• keep penal law alive + keep punish People that actually smart.

what does 4.16 mean?

• do not think only of yourself.

What does 15-21 mean?

• Do not discipline others, discipline yourself.

and provided prompting, cueing, and explaining/modeling support, as Chris had done with summarizing leveled short stories. A key difference was that since Will's groups were more heterogeneous, he had no clear "first" groups to check in with and instead circulated the room, listening in on conversations until the opportunities for asking those first probing questions availed themselves. Each time students met in these groups, Will was prepared with a few questions specific to that day's analects that he could ask as a way to check for understanding, actively trying to move beyond the common default mode of being merely "available help" when students perceived themselves as stuck.

After this five-day cycle of instruction, activity, assessment, and response (including trying to break students of a new pattern Will saw—responding to only one part of an analect if it was lengthy), it was time for students to tackle the performance task. Because he knew that students were still at varying levels of competence, Will built tiers, or leveled checkpoints, into the assessment that allowed students to reveal their current level of development. Students interpreted the analects one at a time before composing the memo to a politician that applied the analects to a real-world issue (see Figures 3.17–3.19). As you can see from the sample student work, some students got only as far as the interpretation of the individual analects, while others were ready to move on to the written synthesis activity. In either case, increased accuracy, confidence, and sophistication were evident in every student's work.

Still, there are clear differences in the students' performances, many of which were predictable based on their work in the preassessment and the short period in which they had to develop new skill and content knowledge related to interpretation of analects. The question of grading, then, immediately comes to the fore. Does Elizabeth deserve a higher grade for her more sophisticated performance on the summative assessment (Figure 3.18), in spite of her more sophisticated performance on the preassessment? Does Maria deserve a low grade for responding to only three of the analects (Figure 3.17), despite the obvious growth since her preassessment—including, importantly, the increased confidence evident in the absence of question marks after every response? And what of Derron (Figure 3.19), who misunderstood the structure of the task but still revealed new understanding?

Initially, Will was prepared to use a rubric to provide both feedback and a grade on this task. The startlingly different ways in which students responded to it—how each in his or her own way demonstrated that he or she was responding significantly to the instruction and feedback Will provided—kept him from doing so. In the late fall semester clamor, Will decided that he was unable at this point to think through sufficiently what the varying levels of student performance on the analects actually meant, so he didn't use grades on this task to measure students'

This excerpt from the SARW captures in all of its complexity the conflict in Will's evaluation and grading dilemma. As you read it, reflect on the way you balance institutional needs for succinct feedback in the form of grades with the full knowledge you have about each of your students.

> When teachers write report cards [or, I contend, assign a grade to any literacy task], they are faced with difficult language decisions. They must find words to represent a student's literate development in all its complexity, often within severe time, space, and format constraints. . . . Some teachers are faced with reducing extensive and complex knowledge about each student's development to a single word or letter. This situation confronts them with very difficult ethical dilemmas. Indeed, the greater the knowledge the teacher has of the student's literacy, the more difficult this task becomes. (p. 8)

Add to this the SARW's acknowledgment that assessment "must take into consideration the differences between basic and academic language [quite pronounced in Will's assignment] and the length of time students need to become skilled at each" (p. 21) [Will knew this was an issue as well] and you'll understand why Will chose to abstain from grading this task, despite its appearance to students as a "test."

Figure 3.17: Maria's work on the performance task.

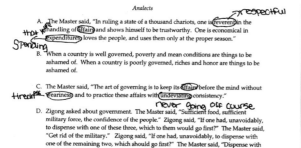

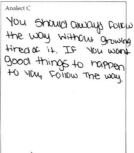

achievement in the "official sense." I respected his decision immensely, as it's a difficult place for teachers to find themselves. He was actively developing his sense of formative assessment and the range of instructional responses it implies, just as the students were developing their sense of how to take up the feedback they got from him in response to the work they produced.

Rather than translating students' performances to a number or letter in the grade book, Will gave himself permission to use the information he gained from the performance task to focus his review instruction for the district-level unit exam and for the semester exam, at this point only days away. The complicated relationships between assessment, instruction, and grades manifested clearly in this scenario, a topic I revisit in the final chapter of the book, where I explore how the vision of assessment embodied in the SARW can drive and inform conversations between multiple partners in the educational process.

Figure 3.18: Elizabeth's work on the performance task.

You are an advisor to an American politician who is considering a run for the Presidency in 2012. The politician has asked you to review influential thinking on government from different cultural and historical figures, and you found this collection of Confucian analects particularly interesting.

Your task is to choose some of the most important or interesting ideas from the analects and write a memo to your candidate explaining what you've learned and how you feel it would be useful advice for a contemporary American national leader.

- First, think through each analect carefully and write a brief paraphrase in the appropriate box on the sheet provided. **Remember to paraphrase the analects from a Confucian perspective;** don't let your modern American point of view influence the ideas the analects express.

- Circle any words you don't know and ask for clarification on their meanings.

- Try to refer to all or parts of all four of the analects in your memo, making note of advice that you think applies to contemporary America. Include references to specific real-world problems and issues to show how the advice is relevant or useful.

- If possible, include discussion of the five relationships and/or the Way to demonstrate your understanding of the analects.

Analects

A. The Master said, "In ruling a state of a thousand chariots, one is reverent in the handling of affairs and shows himself to be trustworthy. One is economical in expenditures, loves the people, and uses them only at the proper season."

B. When a country is well governed, poverty and mean conditions are things to be ashamed of. When a country is poorly governed, riches and honor are things to be ashamed of.

C. The Master said, "The art of governing is to keep its affairs before the mind without weariness, and to practice these affairs with undeviating consistency."

D. Zigong asked about government. The Master said, "Sufficient food, sufficient military force, the confidence of the people." Zigong said, "If one had, unavoidably, to dispense with one of these three, which to them would go first?" The Master said, "Get rid of the military." Zigong said, "If one had, unavoidably, to dispense with one of the remaining two, which should go first?" The Master said, "Dispense with the food. Since ancient time there has hallways been death, but without confidence a people cannot stand."

Analect A

When you rule alot of people, you respect their problems and show they can trust you. You save money, love your people, and only use what you saved at an appropriate time.

Analect B

If you have a good government but there is still poverty in the country then you should be ashamed. If you have a bad government and some people are rich, they should be ashamed for not trying to help their country

All have to do with ruler - ruled relationship

Analect C

The key to ruling is keeping the peoples problems before your own without struggling and to practice putting their problems before your own without letting your problems come before theirs at all

Analect D

In the government, you want plenty of food for the people, a good military, and the peoples confidence. When asked in what order would he get rid of these three things the ruler said first the military because he'd rather have food for his people and their confidence and next he would take the food because confidence in your ruler is like a stable ground

Dear Candidate,

I have been studying Confucious and his knowledge on ruling and I think you will find some of the information very useful.

When ruling many people you need to think more for the people than for yourself. If your government is thriving but there are still homeless people and people with needs than you should be ashamed and try harder to give all people benefits and hom It is important to gain the peoples trust. You want a good army to protect your people, you want plenty of food so they don't starve, but the most important thing when ruling a nation is knowing that the people you rule trust you. sending more troops to Iraq and Vietnam is not helping you gain trust.

I hope you find this information useful and have a good run

Good luck

Figure 3.19: Derron's work on the performance task.

You are an advisor to an American politician who is considering a run for the Presidency in 2012. The politician has asked you to review influential thinking on government from different cultural and historical figures, and you found this collection of Confucian analects particularly interesting.

Your task is to choose some of the most important or interesting ideas from the analects and write a memo to your candidate explaining what you've learned and how you feel it would be useful advice for a contemporary American national leader.

- First, think through each analect carefully and write a brief paraphrase in the appropriate box on the sheet provided. **Remember to paraphrase the analects from a Confucian perspective;** don't let your modern American point of view influence the ideas the analects express.

- Circle any words you don't know and ask for clarification on their meanings.

- Try to refer to all or parts of all four of the analects in your memo, making note of advice that you think applies to contemporary America. Include references to specific real-world problems and issues to show how the advice is relevant or useful.

- If possible, include discussion of the five relationships and/or the Way to demonstrate your understanding of the analects.

Analects

A. The Master said, "In ruling a state of a thousand chariots, one is reverent in the handling of affairs and shows himself to be trustworthy. One is economical in expenditures, loves the people, and uses them only at the proper season."
   Use money carefully respect when you do
B. When a country is well governed, poverty and mean conditions are things to be ashamed of. When a country is poorly governed, riches and honor are things to be ashamed of. *Do not brag about riches; try to reduce poverty*
C. The Master said, "The art of governing is to keep its affairs before the mind without weariness, and to practice these affairs with undeviating consistency." *Keep working on government affairs*
D. Zigong asked about government. The Master said, "Sufficient food, sufficient military force, the confidence of the people." Zigong said, "If had, unavoidably, to dispense with one of these three, which to them would go first?" The Master said, "Get rid of the military." Zigong said, "If one had, unavoidably, to dispense with one of the remaining two, which should go first?" The Master said, "Dispense with the food. Since ancient time there has hallways been death, but without confidence a people cannot stand." *Government is based on confidence in people*

Analect A To ___:
One can learn a lot from Master Confucius. According to Analect A, you should always use money carefully. I'm sure you already know this. Respect the ~~Presid~~ Presidency its the most important Job.

Analect B to ___ :
the most important point about ruling a country is to keep the country is to keep the country out of depressions + reduce Poverty, Ignore the modern studdies of the economy. Instead stdy the economis of the great depression. they are proven to work.

Analect C TO ___ :
Ruling the United States is not a tiny job. You will feel like quitting. keep working its important.

Analect D TO ___ :
try to educate the people, and listen to the polls. democracies do not work if you dout if people loose trust in you, your political career is over.

Tools for Thought from Chapter 3

This chapter offers a view of formative assessment within a specific framework for instruction, the gradual release of responsibility. Whether or not you, your department, or your school is interested in pursuing study of this model, the lessons it offers about assessment are valuable.

- Careful assessment along clearly identified learning goals is the basis for differentiated instruction. Temporarily grouping students based on assessment information and providing those groups with different texts or different activities to do with text is a way to meet students' needs.

- That said, grouping is only one instructional response to assessment information. Using think-alouds to show students new ways of responding to text is an effective response when most of the class seems likely to benefit from instruction on a similar skill or strategy.

- Most assessment should be carefully planned to imply the next step of instruction. Assessing for the purpose of generating grades, though a traditional reason for assessment in schools, is neither the only nor necessarily the most effective way to help us achieve our goal of creating more careful and confident readers. Students respond to teacher talk that lets them know their performance on a particular task will help give them the best educational experience we can offer them. The shift away from the "work for points" model seems scary at first, but if you replace the assessment incentive of scores for careful and caring instruction, the students will go with you.

Chapter Four

Beyond "Zenning It": Reflecting on Professional Practice through Reading Assessment

When I visited Nikki Miller's ninth-grade biology class, students were reading and discussing introductory material on DNA as part of their pursuit of the essential question, "How do form and function relate in living things?" Nikki, whose commitment to using assessment to support her students as readers and learners becomes more than evident later in this chapter, explained to students that she would be coming around to join in their conversations. "This is not just about finding the right answer. I want to talk with you about how you're going about finding it," she told them as they moved into groups of two or three around lab tables. "I'm curious about *how* you read science." The similarity of Nikki's language to that of her colleague Faith Sharp (see Chapter 2) is a testament to the power of true professional learning communities, wherein teachers engage in collaborative inquiry into topics such as the discipline-specific nature of reading and writing.

Students took up the task, taking turns reading silently or aloud to one another a text that Nikki had prepared for them by highlighting key content vocabulary and interspersing questions to guide and check their understanding. As I joined Nikki in moving from group to group to listen in and offer occasional guidance, I was struck by this moment of conversation, which at once had nothing and everything to do with the task at hand: "I want to be a lawyer," Brenda explained to her friend, "but I won't because of all that reading. All that time in the book." Her tablemate looked up from her work as Brenda continued. "I can't afford to flunk." I can't imagine a moment that more fully captures the overlap of Kucer's (2008) dimensions of reading (see Chapter 1); students' perceptions of reading, assessment, and self; and the need for teachers to consider seriously their roles in the development of their students as readers.

Though I've been doing so at least implicitly throughout this book, in this chapter I take up very purposefully the SARW's empowering call for an "ethos that educators are learners too" (p. 27). Engaging in quality formative assessment, particularly in the realm of adolescent reading, is pedagogy few of us entered our careers fully prepared to do. Rather, it's something we're constantly in the process of developing a capacity to do—for the benefit of students like Brenda, who should not feel at age fifteen that certain life pathways have been closed off to her, as well as for those students who enter high school already exceedingly well prepared and confident about their abilities as readers and where those abilities can take them. A commitment to all these students—and a shared commitment to one another as a staff—has led the teachers at our school to willingly allow their classrooms and school to become a center of inquiry where "teachers investigate and improve their own . . . teaching practices" (SARW, p. 16).

I use the word *allow* here intentionally, to offer a balance to the SARW's important, but insufficient, declaration of the value of "an investment in staff development and the creation of conditions that enable teachers to reflect on their own practice" (p. 13). One of those unnamed (and perhaps unnameable in any practical sense) "conditions" is developing within teachers the active desire to take on the responsibility of adolescent reading support, a charge that was almost certainly not part of their formal education and does not receive enough attention in job-embedded professional development, even in the most ideal circumstances. Offering collaboration time during the work day and investing in job-embedded professional development through coaching positions such as mine are certainly important, but ultimately it's the teacher's active will to question, change, and improve that leads to gains in student achievement. I'm fortunate to work in a setting that both provides such conditions and happens to employ a great number of educators who have that desire to challenge their own experiential wisdom and expertise by checking it against how students are actually responding to and learning from instruction.

In this chapter, I offer scenes featuring three such teachers, beginning with examples from the classroom of Gary Slotnick, the English teacher whose shifts in assessment beliefs give this chapter its title. Then I share insights from Kathy Decker and her students as they read and discuss the autobiography of Frederick Douglass and begin Ernest J. Gaines's novel *A Lesson Before Dying*. I close by returning to Nikki Miller's grade 9 biology classroom, where Brenda and her classmates are building an understanding of DNA and cellular genetics through reading, writing, and conversation. Together, these examples offer a portrait of teachers at work at developing assessment that, in the words of the SARW, explores

> how the educational environment and the participants in the educational community support the process of students as they learn to become independent and collaborative thinkers and problem solvers. This exploration includes an examination of the environment for teaching and learning, the processes and products of learning, and the degree to which all participants . . . meet their obligation to support inquiry [as an approach to assessment]. Such assessments examine not only learning over time but also the contexts of learning. (p. 2)

By inquiring through and *about* assessment, the teachers in this chapter (who are, after all, central to the learning context of their classrooms) both gain affirming clarity about their role in the classroom and uncover the need for changes in their role and identities in pursuit of the development of their students as readers and thinkers. In other words, these teachers, through their focus on assessment, both questioned and improved their instructional practice.

Gary Slotnick: Reconsidering How to Give Help and Responding to an Administrative Challenge

Gary Slotnick's semester-long senior English class begins with a study of short stories. Gary capitalizes on the brevity and variety of the genre to engage students, to model effective reading and thinking, and to continue to build student understanding of the elements of literature. When we sat down to discuss how he might more purposefully use formative reading assessment with this group—a co-taught class composed of several students with individualized education programs (IEPs), many students with significant motivation and attendance gaps, and most with early-onset senioritis—Gary shared his desire to begin looking more carefully at his students as readers, as well as his concerns. "We've been better at assessing writing, but it's a lot of work to keep track of every kid," he explained, echoing the not-uncommon preference to talk about the more visible process of writing when it comes to assessing adolescent literacy. To let student work guide instructional choices, "initially we [Gary and his PLC colleagues] wanted to look at our student writing holistically, because that's what we've always done. But how do we know we're right? Can we always trust our gut-level response?"

Gary eventually summed up his holistic approach to assessing student writing, explaining that "in the past we've decided that we're going to kind of 'Zen it'"—in other words, trust their expertise as teachers of writing (and as writers themselves)—to help guide full-class instruction in their writing classes. Unfortunately, most secondary teachers don't have a similar "Zen-like" capacity for approaching reading. So Gary and his colleagues decided that this semester they would look more carefully at their students as readers, beginning with a preassessment that combined both content knowledge and process (see Figures 4.1 and 4.2 for the preassessment and two student responses). Ultimately, we came up with three different ways to look at student work in order to give Gary both the high-level view of the classroom's shared strengths and weaknesses and the more fine-grained sense of each student as an individual.

Much as Chris Belt did (see Chapter 3), Gary administered the preassessment by explaining to his students what a preassessment was: "We want to see where you are, see what you guys can already do. We don't want to waste your time covering things we can tell you've already mastered *or* gloss over things we assume you can already do." He then asked them to open their literature books to Kate Chopin's "The Story of an Hour," "the shortest short story you will ever read," Gary told them encouragingly. Students read and responded to seven questions he and his colleagues had written, each designed to get at a content concept (e.g., theme; identification and application of symbolism) or a valued course habit (e.g., making connections; sharing something interesting).

Gary and I met to look at the student work (Figures 4.1 and 4.2, responses from Frank and Isabel) and decided to analyze the preassessment data in three interrelated ways. First, we read each student's responses carefully, taking a high degree of satisfaction in what the students could already do. (Recall my reference in Chapter 3 to Peter Elbow's [1993] use of the term *liking* as a feature of assessment; Elbow argues that we can critique more effectively that which we like.) We used a student versus content goal matrix (see Figure 4.3) to indicate degrees of evident strength and weakness in each concept area for each student. This was the least Zen-like approach because it required us to look carefully at each student's response in relation to the content or process goal it addressed. Taking this approach gave Gary a fine-grained view of what each of his students could do with one piece of text. He was aware that this view was merely a snapshot of performance—one reading of one text on one particular late summer morning—but it gave him a solid start on knowing each of his students as readers of the kind of literature they would be exposed to in the class. As the SARW caution, we can't do much generalization from this one look, since "characteristics of the text, the task, the situation, and the purpose can all have an impact on the student's performance, and only some aspects of reading and writing will be captured in any given assessment" (p. 19).

Figure 4.1: Frank's preassessment.

Short Story Unit Pretest

Directions: Please read the short story and answer the following questions as thoroughly as you can. Please use complete sentences so that your intended meaning is understood.

1) What do you think is a main idea or theme of this story?
   a crazy women who thinks something is out to get her

2) Give one example of an image (use one of your senses) from this story.
   a ugly disgusting hand coming down to grab her

3) Give one example of a symbol from the story, and tell what it represents.

4) Give one example of irony from the story, and explain why it is ironic.

5) How is a short story different from larger works? (And don't say, "It's shorter.")
   a short story has less detailes than a larger story

6) What is a connection between this story and something else that you have read or watched?
   Devil may cry the serious not the anime

7) Explain anything else from the story that you don't understand, or that you really understand well (impress me), or anything else that you found interesting about the story.
   why is she crazy

Figure 4.2: Isabel's preassessment.

Short Story Unit Pretest

Directions: Please read the short story and answer the following questions as thoroughly as you can. Please use complete sentences so that your intended meaning is understood.

1) What do you think is a main idea or theme of this story?

I think it would be the Death of mrs mallards hoshanb thuy tricke her into thinking her hushans was pea b

2) Give one example of an image (use one of your senses) from this story.

mrs mallard sitting in her room in front of her window expressing her sadhess twords the Death of her husban b

3) Give one example of a symbol from the story, and tell what it represents.

the womans tears repersented sadhess

4) Give one example of irony from the story, and explain why it is ironic.

5) How is a short story different from larger works? (And don't say, "It's shorter.")

well i think it would Be that in short stoays thuy Dont realiy go into to much betail anb in longir ons thuy Do

6) What is a connection between this story and something else that you have read or watched?

well this story is similar to romeo anb Joliet connectab with the beaths in both stories how misunberstaubgs can leab to changes in peo Ples lites

7) Explain anything else from the story that you don't understand, or that you really understand well (impress me), or anything else that you found interesting about the story.

I think the enbing of the, story was intresting because no one kew that the hosLanb woulb be alive anb the woma Deab

As we talked about each student's responses and made an initial judgment about whether the student displayed an applied understanding of each of the literary concepts students would be studying in the semester-long course, Gary made a mark indicating the student's level of performance on the chart in Figure 4.3. Beginning with this fine-grained approach led us through a number of steps that eventually allowed us to think about both the student and the class more holistically, as Gary was accustomed to doing.

As we completed this step for each student, we created a quick individual summary of each student's more general competence in applied understanding of the literary terms and ability to communicate his or her thinking about a text. We also composed a brief commentary regarding a strength and a demonstrated weakness for each student (see Figure 4.4). Together, these processes brought us to what used to be Gary's starting point—a more Zen-like approach to holistic scoring. Only now were we able to record with strong confidence the number of students who "Get it/Don't get it" for the key concepts of the unit, for this particular text. We used the class-level chart in Figure 4.5 to gain a clearer sense of strengths and gaps that might require more focused full-class attention.

This multistep, recursive process took more than one period of Gary's preparatory time, but it prompted in Gary three distinct but highly related responses—all of which suggest the power of assessment to spur professional growth. The first response was more or less what he had intended to happen: he was able to focus more instructional time on the content areas that students needed the most help with, which in this case turned out to be the ability to identify and explain the possible significance of irony and symbolism in a work of literature. As we created the class-level chart and those needs became visibly obvious, Gary also pointed out that he could have predicted those would be the areas of greatest need. Part of Gary's Zen-it philosophy comes from his knowledge of students' general developmental and curricular trajectories; gaps in more abstract and interpretive thinking are highly predictable. The power of the preassessment, he learned, is to let the *students* in on the "Zen" and make it clear that instructional decisions aren't based solely on teachers' gut-level response, but on information the students give us in response to our purposefully designed prompts to seek it out.

Figure 4.3: Student vs. content goal matrix with information for Frank and Isabel included.

Student	Theme	Imagery	Symbolism	Irony
Frank	No	OK	No response	No response
Isabel	No	OK	Yes	No response
Student 3 and so on				

Figure 4.4: Individual student performance summary.

Student: Frank

The student has a strong applied understanding of literary elements/the genre of short story.	4 3 2 **1**
The student is able to communicate connections, confusions, or other thinking about a story.	4 3 **2** 1

A strength and a weakness

+Beginning understanding of short story form, articulated the basis for a connection, asked a clarifying question
−Misreading of main character, likely had trouble accessing/processing the text

Student: Isabel

The student has a strong applied understanding of literary elements/the genre of short story.	4 **3** 2 1
The student is able to communicate connections, confusions, or other thinking about a story.	**4** 3 2 1

A strength and a weakness

+Underlined key terms in questions, good basic summary, fantastic connection
−Irony

Figure 4.5: Tallied summary of individual student performance on each goal. Note: We had to use an un-planned-for "middle column" for main idea/theme because the wording of the question invited students to state the most important plot point as "main idea" (see Isabel's response to this item in Figure 4.2 for an example). This was a minor inconvenience in the scheme of things, but a reminder of the central role of clear, precise questions in assessment.

Goal	Get it	Don't get it
Main idea/theme	| | | | | | | | | |	| | | | | | | |
Imagery	| | | | | | | | | | | |	| | | | |
Symbol/explanation	| | | | | |	| | | | | | | | | | | |
Irony/explanation	| | | | | |	| | | | | | | | | | | |
Short story genre	| | | | | | | | | | | | | | | |	| | | |
Make connections	| | |	| | | | | |
Explain thinking	| | | | | | |	| | |

The SARW challenge us to use assessment to "encourage students to become engaged in literacy learning, to reflect on their own reading and writing in productive ways, and to set respective literacy goals" (p. 11). When an assessment offers insight into particular facets of content knowledge, as did Gary's assessment of applied knowledge of theme, imagery, irony, and symbol, students can set goals for when and how they will demonstrate new understanding of concepts that may initially have been unfamiliar or underdeveloped. An example of such a goal might be: "After reading a challenging short story that I select, I'll be able to identify an example of irony, explain the source of irony, and suggest how the ironic tension adds to the story." See Chapter 5 for an example of such a goal-setting conversation in a conference setting.

Just as the class-level snapshot helped Gary focus instruction, the student-level summaries prompted a second response: tailoring his interventions to individual students as they moved toward completion of the independent assessment. This project asks students to select a short story and engage in a thorough literary analysis of it using a more formalized version of the preassessment, but with more time and student choice helping to fuel motivation. Traditionally, by high school the responsibility for seeking assistance has shifted almost entirely to the student. "If students don't come in after school for help," we explain to ourselves and to others, "then there's not much I can do about it." While there is something sensible in this approach—teens should be taking responsibility for their own learning whenever possible—when teachers know more about their students' strengths and weaknesses as readers, they can counter the problematic aspects of such an approach to helping students by intervening more purposefully within the school day.

In this case, instead of waiting for Frank to ask Gary for help in identifying and interpreting a symbol in the short story he chose to read—or letting him struggle fruitlessly, or ignore the prompt altogether as he did on the preassessment—Gary was able to approach Frank as he worked on his project to ask him how he was doing on the elements that Gary suspected he might struggle with given what the assessment had revealed. Although a significant amount of instruction, assessment, and response had occurred between the preassessment and this final project, the point is the same: when the teacher is aware of a student's needs, those needs can be communicated with the student and can become a point around which one-on-one instruction occurs within the classroom. The information contained in Figure 4.3 became a tool both for charting student development along the content goals and for focusing individualized teacher support through conversation and guidance.

And finally, thoughtful consideration of the information that students had given him in the preassessment prompted Gary to feel a sense of the power inherent in purposefully seeking out the answer to a question he has about students. Though we didn't explicitly frame this experience as inquiry, Gary discovered the underlying truth of what it means to inquire: you can find out the answers only to those questions you ask. Gary offered evidence of this shift in thinking when he shared with excitement some revisions he had made to a study guide on John

Updike's short story "A&P" (see Figure 4.6). The questions he'd been asking on the original study guide were generic—not to disparage them as questions, but rather to describe their function as "questions to see if students are getting it," rather than questions purposefully designed to reveal the kinds of understandings about reading that Gary was coming to value.

The discussion Gary's students had while thinking through these new questions, which are tied more explicitly to the language of the analytical approach Gary was teaching, was impressive. At one point, students revealed a surprising point of mismatch between their background knowledge and the world as Updike writes about it. Not all students picked up on the fact that the protagonist who was bagging the groceries was an employee. In their experience, scanning and bagging is something they see the customer doing just as frequently as a store worker. This role of student background knowledge is a topic I take up more fully in the next section.

Even more significant than the revision of the questions Gary asked on a daily basis to check for student understanding was a project he *did* frame as purposeful inquiry. This inquiry question stemmed from some good-natured challenges Gary was getting from an administrator who, because students at our school

Figure 4.6: Original and revised questions revealing Gary's more focused stance as an assessor.

Items from old study guide	Items from revised study guide
1. Who is Sammy? Describe him. 2. What does Sammy fear about the customers at the A&P? 3. How does Sammy describe the three girls who come into the store? 4. How do those girls differ from the usual customers of the A&P? 5. Who is Lengel? What happens when he comes out of his office? 6. What does Sammy think Queenie's home life is like? What makes him think that? 7. How does Sammy's home life compare to Queenie's? 8. How does Sammy perceive Queenie feels about the people who work at the A&P? 9. What does Sammy do toward the end of the story? Why? 10. Why does Sammy claim the world was going to be hard for him hereafter?	1. Use two words to describe Sammy's traits. 2. Use two words to describe Sammy's circumstances. 3. How does Sammy describe the three girls who come into the store? 4. Did you list traits or circumstances? Why do you think you did so? 5. |	Queenie's home life	Sammy's home life
---	---	---
Supporting text		
Describe in your own words		
Who/what is the source of this info?			 6. Why does the source of the information in question 5 matter? 7. Why does Sammy *really* quit his job? 8. What is a possible theme of this story? 9. Questions? Opinions? Comments? Something you understood? Something you realized? Something you are confused about?

read *Romeo and Juliet* as ninth graders, *Macbeth* as sophomores, and *Hamlet* as seniors, wondered why we asked our students to read so much Shakespeare—and questioned whether, by the time they were seniors, students were able to read and comprehend Shakespeare's complex text any better than they had when they were ninth graders.

While we might have relied on the playwright whose work we were concerned with to supply the question—essentially, "To be, or not to be?"—Gary and I instead devised our own question: How much better can academic-level students read and understand Shakespeare independently better after instruction than before? Implicit in this question are consequent questions of pedagogy: What are the teaching methods and habits that seem to contribute to an improved level of motivation and achievement? What new approaches does the student work suggest might be appropriate?

To that end, Gary chose a sonnet that resonates with some of the themes and language of *Hamlet* and asked his students to read and paraphrase or summarize it independently. His students didn't take up this task as willingly as they had reading Chopin's short story some weeks earlier. The text was richer, denser, more compact—and, we suspect, students have been lead to believe, through both intentional and unintentional practices, that they *cannot* read Shakespeare on their own. Some of the written responses were blank, but many students gave a strong effort, as Tanisha's writing in Figure 4.7 demonstrates. Notice that she chooses to take on the "I" of the persona and paraphrases line by line, and that her analysis reveals a basically literal interpretation ("the disease" = "getting over a cold" and missing "My reason" as the referent of "his prescriptions"). In the couplet, though, Tanisha reveals a key understanding—that the speaker feels a disconnect between his assessment of his love and her true characteristics.

As part of their final assessment on *Hamlet*, after much in-class reading and discussion both of the play and how to read the play, students saw the same sonnet, but this time with more context. Gary told them, "This sonnet is an example of one that might have been written by Hamlet as one of his letters to Ophelia," before asking them to summarize or paraphrase the sonnet again. On the second reading (see Figure 4.8), Tanisha takes a different stance—one that does obscure possible misunderstandings, to be sure, but that we felt revealed even more understanding. Most noticeably, Tanisha takes a step back to discuss the poem as a whole, not taking on the persona's "I" and not taking a line-by-line approach. While it would be useful to know *why* she feels the text suggests the speaker is "in love with someone they shouldn't be in love with," and to get a sense of the degree to which the metaphors contributed to or muddled understanding, we were left with a sense that Tanisha does indeed feel comfortable and confident in approaching the text.

Tanisha's response to the follow-up question, "Why do you think Hamlet

Figure 4.7: Tanisha's preassessment sonnet response.

Translation to Modern English Pre-Assessment

Directions: Translate the following text into modern English, either line by line or idea by idea.

My love is as a fever, longing still	I'm still in love with you.
For that which longer nurseth the disease,	I'm still getting over a cold
Feeding on that which doth preserve the ill,	I ~~get fed~~ ate something bad.
Th' uncertain sickly appetite to please.	I live to please
My reason, the physician to my love,	
Angry that his prescriptions are not kept,	I'm mad b/c you don't keep your promises.
Hath left me, and I desperate now approve	
Desire is death, which physic did except.	
Past cure I am, now reason is past care,	I'm too far gone
And frantic mad with evermore unrest;	I'm going crazy w/ sleepless nights.
My thoughts and my discourse as madmen's are,	
At random from the truth vainly express'd;	
For I have sworn thee fair, and thought thee bright,	You're not who I thought you were
Who art as black as hell, as dark as night	who is evil

would have written this to Ophelia?," suggests a fairly sophisticated level of under-standing, as she points out (first rather generally) that it could be a direct address to Ophelia as an expression of his true feelings, *but also* that it could be an attempt on Hamlet's behalf to get Polonius to "think Hamlet's crazy because of his love for Ophelia." Again, the direct connections between the text and the student's inter-pretations are not evident, but Tanisha's work affirmed Gary's efforts to engage students in the study of complex literature such as *Hamlet*.

Though in some ways Gary's use of assessment might seem incongruous with the SARW's admonition to de-emphasize assessment as a means of "prov[ing] whether . . . learning has taken place" (p. 16), Gary's Shakespeare inquiry actually extends well beyond such a narrow focus. In the spirit of critical inquiry into cur-riculum and instruction (Standard 4), Gary was in some ways seeking to address the SARW's concern with the potential for assessment to lead to

> students being placed in different instructional settings . . . with the intention of producing a better match between student and curriculum. . . . On the one hand, a better instructional match is possible, but on the other, different and perhaps lowered expectations on the parts of both teachers and students themselves may result. (p. 21)

Figure 4.8: Tanisha's paraphrase of the poem after instruction.

Modern Translation: The following sonnet (poem) is an example of one that might have been written by Hamlet as one of his letters to Ophelia. **Translate** the poem into **modern English,** either line by line or idea by idea. **(20 points)**

My love is as a fever, longing still

For that which longer nurseth the disease,

Feeding on that which doth preserve the ill,

Th' uncertain sickly appetite to please.

My reason, the physician to my love,

Angry that his prescriptions are not kept,

Hath left me, and I desperate now approve

Desire is death, which physic did except.

Past cure I am, now reason is past care,

And frantic mad with evermore unrest;

My thoughts and my discourse as madmen's are,

At random from the truth vainly express'd;

For I have sworn thee fair, and thought thee bright,

Who art as black as hell, as dark as night

> The person who was writing this is saying that they are in love with someone they shouldn't be in love with, and they are confused about it because the person doesn't love them back.

Why do you think Hamlet would have written this to Ophelia? He could have written it to Ophelia because he really is in love with her, or for Polonius' eyes, so he'll think Hamlet's crazy because of his love for Ophelia.

Keenly aware of the potential inequities that come with academic tracking by assessed ability levels (Gary's class is the lowest of three tracks at the senior year), Gary was seeking validation for the time and effort it takes to read a text as challenging as *Hamlet* with students in his academic-level class. He was able to take student work from his inquiry project to the questioning administrator and talk with him about students such as Tanisha and the kinds of work Gary did with them to develop the capacity to read and respond to Shakespeare independently.

To be sure, the students in Gary's Advanced Placement class, who read and summarized the same sonnet on their end-of-unit assessment, giving Gary a means of comparison, could do so with more sophistication and confidence than the students in Tanisha's class could. But if we allow ourselves to take, as the SARW suggest, a developmental rather than merely mastery approach to reading, we can see that Tanisha responded to the sonnet with as much accuracy of interpretation and more confidence than she'd had before reading *Hamlet*. Even more important—since, of course, not every student demonstrated such growth—Gary developed some instructional cues for the next time he approaches *Hamlet* with students, specifically

- modeling how he thinks through the effect of considering possible meanings of multimeaning words (for example, *reason* in line 5) and
- calling explicit attention to the basic structure of subject-verb-object when considering syntax in a close reading (for example, "My reason" serving as the subject for "hath left me" despite the intervening phrases).

Both of these reading processes are largely invisible when a skilled reader of Shakespeare relies only on his "Zen" approach to assessment. When teachers don't pay attention to the specific elements of what it means to read a difficult text, they can't truly know what students need to learn. Looking carefully at student work, created in

One of the most rewarding aspects of teaching is knowing that you have another chance to try something or to continue perfecting a lesson or approach. The SARW encourage us to "use assessment to reflect on learning and teaching but also to examine, constantly and critically, the assessment process itself and its relation to instruction" (p. 16). A valuable follow-up activity to Gary's postassessment would be to give students their preassessment side by side with their postassessment and have them discuss and/or write reflectively about how their understanding and ability to interpret the language of the sonnet changed.

Based on what you've read in this or previous chapters, consider an activity, assignment, or assessment you'll give yourself the freedom to try differently the next time around.

Gary's work with assessment helped him to clarify and redefine his role as instructor in the classroom, a topic I take up in the next section as well. By gaining a clearer sense of what each of his students needed, Gary could preempt their need to ask for help, instead approaching them directly to seek evidence of their ability to do or understand something, or provide assistance if they still needed it. Assessment doesn't reduce the number of roles you may have to fill in a classroom, but it does help you know a bit more clearly which role(s) you need to play with which students when they most need it.

response to purposefully developed questions and prompts, was a significant means for allowing Gary to go beyond Zen to meet very real and specific student needs.

Kathy Decker: Assessing Background Knowledge and Reconsidering Teacher as Questioner

In my account of Gary's classroom, the central role of background knowledge—the content-specific and "world-general" information our students bring to text—became obvious when students expressed confusion over checking out and bagging groceries as a signifier of employment at the grocery store. There is good reason to believe that the level of background knowledge a reader brings to text is the single greatest facilitator of comprehension of that text. Gary could not have known this would happen and could not have prepared students for such confusion; the supportive conversations with peers and with him were enough to work through the mismatch between the story's schema for "grocery store" and that which some students brought to the text.

In contrast, when Kathy Decker began preparing to read *Narrative of the Life of Frederick Douglass, an American Slave* with her academic-level juniors, she knew her students would be bringing with them a great deal of background knowledge about the general topic of the text, an African American man's experiences in and escape from slavery, but that this knowledge would be uneven. To build from students' stores of background knowledge and to identify areas in which Kathy might need to do some work, she and her colleagues developed an anticipation guide (Figure 4.9) consisting of several statements written in response to these criteria (adapted from Fisher & Frey, 2009):

- What background information or concepts are foundational to understanding the book?

- What conceptual aspects of the book will require multiple exposures to develop?

- What misconceptions do students have that may get in the way of understanding the book?

Kathy presented the activity to the class as something "like a survey," which piqued students' interest, since she was implying that what they thought mattered—which, in her class, it does—and that the stakes were low. The anticipation guide encouraged Kathy's students to willingly reveal gaps in background knowledge and to discuss them with the rest of the class, which meant Kathy didn't have to address them obliquely herself. Using this chart to preassess student background knowledge represents a shift in the way new content is sometimes presented in class. Teachers often have a sense (that "Zenning it" approach again) of what

Figure 4.9: An anticipation guide for *Narrative of the Life of Frederick Douglass, an American Slave.*

Statement	Strongly agree/ Very likely true	Agree/ Probably true	Disagree/ Probably not true	Strongly disagree/ Very likely not true
1. Slavery was much the same wherever one was. There were few differences in slave life on plantations in the South compared to houses in the cities.				
Explain your thinking:				
2. Education can sometimes work both for and against people. Sometimes, the more a person learns, the more painful the world becomes.				
Explain your thinking:				
3. An autobiography is always 100% true.				
Explain your thinking:				
4. Individuals within an oppressed group all handle the oppression in the same way.				
Explain your thinking:				
5. Many slaveowners used the Christian religion to justify slavery.				
Explain your thinking:				

students' strengths and weaknesses are—even without checking—and therefore proceed to apply the background knowledge treatment, through lecture or PowerPoint, without precise knowledge of what students *actually* know and think.

Useful as this preassessment tool is for demonstrating how teachers can rethink their role in building background knowledge to support comprehension, this is not the most significant story I want to tell about Kathy's shift in practice brought about through assessment. Kathy is a masterful questioner. As I watched her lead a class discussion about Frederick Douglass, she skillfully and seamlessly ramped up the level of complexity of thought from a basic plot question that verified understanding to a question about "Why?" or "So what?" Students were primarily acting as responders to Kathy's questions, but as they began reading Chapter 8 of Douglass's narrative, a student asked a question of his own: "How do you put a price on somebody?" Kathy was able to use this student's question both to further their larger discussion on humanity and oppression as well as to focus the reading for that particular section of text.

After this class period, I mentioned to Kathy that I noticed she was asking all these fantastic questions and students were responding thoughtfully to them, but wouldn't it be great if *they* were asking more of the questions like the one the student shared toward the end of class. My question to her, intended as a quick hallway comment, was more unsettling than I intended it to be. "Yeah," she said, "but asking questions like that is the most fun part of my job. I feel like it *is* my job."

Kathy is certainly right. Knowing her content as well as she does allows her to ask the right questions to get her students thinking about the critical aspects of the texts they study. She is expert at generating informal

> assessment information in classrooms . . . made available in students' talk about their reading. . . . When students have conversations about a book, for instance, a teacher hears the process of their comprehending. Unless a teacher can generate such conversations among children, this information is simply not available. (SARW, p. 14).

Kathy's students were offering up information through their answers that helped her to assess their levels of understanding, but only through unplanned student questioning did she get a sense of what *they* were wondering or thinking about. Kathy and I became interested in how she could generate questioning and active participation from students, shifting some of the responsibility for inquiry away from Kathy and onto the students themselves. To help her better gauge her students' ability to question and participate actively in the classroom, I shared a modified version of a tool I'd used in my own classes (see Figure 4.10). I had found it helpful, first, to describe for students what thoughtful and effective participation looks like (an aspect of construct validity, as discussed in Chapter 2) and to make students aware of and responsible for their own level of engagement in class.

Before sharing the chart with students, Kathy had them simply write a question on a slip of paper at the end of class after reading the first chapter of Ernest Gaines's *A Lesson Before Dying*. At the beginning of the next class, she selected a few of their questions that helped to demonstrate the distinction between clarifying and wondering and then offered students supportive feedback for asking the kinds of questions that she'd be asking anyway. In fact, students asked the question "What does it mean to be a man?" on their own—one of the central questions Kathy and her colleagues planned on having the students inquire about.

Figure 4.10: Participation self-awareness chart.

During reading today, I contributed to the quality of the group's understanding of the novel by . . .	Keep a tally here
Asking a clarifying question (There was something I didn't understand that I knew I needed to "get" to keep following along.)	
Asking a wondering question (I understood what the author meant, but it made me wonder about a significant issue.)	
Making an observation or interpretation (I made a meaningful connection or noticed something significant about what the author was trying to say.)	
Sharing a thoughtful emotional response (The novel made me feel a certain way that either helped me understand or was getting in the way of understanding.)	
Answering a question/responding to an observation (from a classmate or Mrs. Decker)	
On the reverse, write something you wish you had asked or shared during reading today.	

From there, Kathy was able to talk through the purposes of the chart, making sure that students understood that the precise labeling of the question or response was not nearly as important as engaging in the classroom conversation about the literature and keeping track of their participation throughout the week. Although Kathy eschews charts and graphic organizers for their unnaturalness, one of her many great traits, daily completion of and weekly reflection on the participation chart is a clear example of "routines for systematic assessment in order to ensure that each student is benefiting optimally from instruction" (SARW, p. 14). Students are encouraged to participate thoughtfully, and Kathy is free to continue to be an active participant in the conversation since the responsibility for recording participation is theirs, not hers. Not only did paying attention to the way her students responded to what they'd read allow Kathy to make an effective change in practice, but the tool we designed also became an ongoing source of informal assessment as students became more comfortable with their role as generator of questions in the classroom.

Like Gary, Kathy saw anew the position she needed to take in her classroom, not just *because* of assessment evidence, but also for the sake of providing the "space" for generating it. When a school truly embraces inquiry—as its approach not just to assessment but also to teaching and learning more broadly—everyone needs practice in taking the active role of asking questions to propel thinking and explore meaning. Giving students a tool that reminds them of the discussion behaviors we prize in English class, prompts them to engage in those behaviors, and allows them to record and self-assess their success at displaying the behaviors is a good example of curriculum, instruction, and assessment overlapping, as they ideally should. Consider how often you ask students to generate their own questions about what they've read. How do you assess the questions they ask and the discussion those questions prompt?

Nikki Miller: Assessing Is in Her Genes

Everywhere I looked in Nikki Miller's biology classroom (which I described briefly at the beginning of this chapter), I could see and hear evidence of the centrality of formative assessment in the way she structured her teaching and the way students understood their learning. On most days, students began the period by writing in their notebooks in response to a prompt (e.g., How does an organism's ability to respond to its environment help it to stay alive?), allowing Nikki to check their understanding of previous learning, discover gaps in understanding, and prepare the class for the new content ahead.

Just before the class period in which I overheard Brenda voice her lack of confidence about reading to her classmate, Nikki gave students an envelope that contained images of cell parts on some cards and the names of the cell parts on the others. The students' task was to match the image with the name and create a book in which they also wrote about the function of that component within the cell. As students worked on this, I asked them how they knew which images matched with which labels. "I tried to think of the model project with all the parts," said one student. "I studied a little bit that night," he confessed. "Yesterday we did a packet to help us understand and define everything," said another student. "We drew pictures." Almost every student I talked to could remember where in the learning process his or her knowledge and understanding came from. Learning activities (from the students' perspective) and assessment activities (from Nikki's perspective) were happily blurred, but clarity about the content itself and who was responsible for learning it was obvious.

Later, I shared with Nikki how impressed I was at the way formative assessment functioned in her class. Knowing my interest in collaborating with her on formative reading assessment, she blurted out, "But I feel we're getting so much away from reading!" The information she was gathering about students from labs, projects, and experiments was giving her the information she needed to guide instruction. "But I'm not sure about teaching content reading skills. I don't want to take them out, but just doing questions . . . Is that assessment?" This conversation revealed Nikki's thoughtfulness about the function of questioning, her desire to maintain reading as a central component of students' learning experiences, and her concern about the time it can take to teach content area reading. Our plan for addressing all of this was simple: we would watch as students read and answered the questions about DNA (the ones I mentioned at the beginning of the chapter) and then review their work to determine what the next step should be.

This reading activity is what I call "first draft" reading; Nikki used it to introduce some of the major concepts and vocabulary associated with DNA. As such, we didn't expect perfection in students' responses, nor did their ability to answer the questions about the reading mean they actually understood everything they wrote. This kind of reading challenges students to work through new content in ways that are often expected in academic settings—a solid college-readiness habit—and sets the stage for other learning activities that will extend and reinforce the nascent understandings developed through reading.

As we looked through student work, the answer to Nikki's question "Is 'doing questions' assessment?" became clear: if she responded in some meaningful way to students' reading processes, then yes, its role as a learning activity extended to the additional role of formative assessment. Her other concern, finding time to teach reading strategies, was answered as well. Her instructional response was to challenge the ineffective strategies or stances we saw consistently in student responses. Though the SARW caution us to use assessment to "emphasize what students can do rather than what they cannot do" (p. 11), they also acknowledge that when handled skillfully, "information about students' confusions, counterproductive strategies, and limitations . . . can help students and teachers reflect on and learn about students' reading" (p. 12).

Take, for example, Marcus's response to question 15 in Figure 4.11. When asked, "What is meant by the 'base pair' rule?," he responded, as did many of his classmates, with the sentence that immediately followed the term in bold in the text before question 13. Nikki saw in this error the opportunity not only to clarify the science concept, but also to clear up the obvious student misconception about textbook reading—that the definition of a term always follows it. When she projected the related paragraph on the screen the next day, she combined a read-aloud with instruction on "reading for understanding versus reading to get it done." She clarified the misconception, reinforced by textbooks that almost always follow the "new term → definition" pattern, and then challenged students to think about how they could have known that this answer was incorrect. "How could we check to see if that answer makes sense?" Nikki challenged the students. Eventually a student noticed that Marcus's answer—"can occur in any order along a strand of DNA"—doesn't sound all that much like a rule. "If it's about pairs and rules, 'any order' doesn't make sense," the student went on. Nikki verified this student's response and took the opportunity to point out the function of the signal phrase "This is known as" to refer the reader *back* to the previous content to apply the label.

Maya's response to question 22 in Figure 4.12 reveals a similar gap in both understanding of the science content and the way questions work in an academic setting. Nikki shared the common incorrect response, "The sequence determines which proteins are made," and asked students to figure out what went wrong. A

Figure 4.11: Marcus's response to item 15.

The rungs of the ladder are pairs of 4 types of *nitrogen bases*.   The bases are known by their coded letters A, G, T, C. These bases always bond in a certain way. *Adenine* will only bond to *thymine*. *Guanine* will only bond with *cytosine*. This is known as the *"Base-Pair Rule"*. The bases can occur in any order along a strand of DNA. The order of these bases is the code that contains the instructions. For instance ATGCACATA would code for a different gene than AATTACGGA. A strand of DNA contains millions of bases. *Note that the bases attach to the sides of the ladder at the sugars and not at the phosphate.*

13. What are the rungs of the DNA ladder made of?

4 types of nitrogen

14. What do the following letter abbreviations (for the rungs) stand for?

A: *Adenine*

G: *Guanine*

T: *Thymine*

C: *Cytosine*

15. What is meant by the "base-pair" rule?

Can occur any order doing a strand of DNA.

student happily identified the source of the problem: "They just copied down something from the second sentence!" Nikki capitalized on this student's response to address another set of misconceptions about textbook reading—that questions are always evenly distributed throughout a selection and asked in the order in which the content is presented.

This fifteen-minute mini-lesson will not relieve Brenda, the young woman who didn't want to go to law school because of "all that reading," of her fear of school-based reading, nor does it fully answer Nikki's concerns about her responsibility to support Brenda while also addressing the curriculum content she's obligated to teach. Similarly, Kathy's students did not develop into self-sufficient inquiring readers overnight, and Gary's seniors did not produce perfect explications of a Shakespeare sonnet after reading *Hamlet*. Students did, however, learn considerable lessons—both about the content under study and the processes they used to develop understanding of that content. At the heart of this student learning were the inquiry stances these teachers adopted toward assessment, "promot[ing]

Figure 4.12: Maya's response to item 22.

Messenger RNA

So, now, we know the nucleus controls the cell's activities through the chemical DNA, but how? It is the sequence of bases that determine which protein is to be made. The sequence is like a code that we can now interpret. The sequence determines which proteins are made and the proteins determine which activities will be performed. And that is how the nucleus is the control center of the cell. The only problem is that the DNA is too big to go through the nuclear pores. So a chemical is used to "read" the DNA in the nucleus. That chemical is *messenger RNA*. The messenger RNA (mRNA) is small enough to go through the nuclear pores. It takes the "message" of the DNA to the ribosomes and "tells them" what proteins are to be made. Recall that proteins are the body's building blocks. Imagine that the code taken to the ribosomes is telling the ribosome what is needed - like a recipe.

22. Why doesn't the DNA go to the cytoplasm itself to control the making of proteins?

The sequence determines which proteins are made

23. What chemical is used to "read" the DNA in the nucleus?

RNA

24. Where is the "message" of DNA taken?

To the Ribsomes

problem posing and problem solving as goals for all participants in the educational community" (SARW, p. 2).

This chapter focused very purposefully on the role of teachers in bringing together curriculum, instruction, and assessment. If there is hope for assessment to lead to improved student learning, such effective assessment has to start in the classroom with teachers asking smart questions that prompt them to see themselves and their work—and their students and *their* work—in new, challenging, and exciting ways. As powerful as classroom-based teacher inquiry into assessment

Nikki's work with assessment has less to do with rethinking her role within the classroom discourse structure—as opposed to Gary, who saw the benefit in approaching students to help rather than waiting for them to ask for help, and Kathy, who saw a way to get students to share some of the responsibility for generating questions about literature—and more to do with her ability to take run-of-the-mill assessment (comprehension questions) and turn it into dynamic formative assessment. Aware that her students are not simply receptacles for content knowledge, but rather active participants in the construction of understanding, Nikki looked for opportunities to support the development of processes, habits, and strategies that respect her students' role as young people with growing responsibility for the way they read and learn.

Look at the last set of questions *your* students answered in response to reading. Are there patterns of misinterpretation that invite the sort of modeling and discussion that Nikki engaged in?

is—and I can attest to its power in transforming my instruction, not to mention improving teaching and learning in the classrooms I've described in this and preceding chapters—assessment is bigger than any one classroom. Making assessment work, fairly and effectively, for *all* of our students requires the shared commitment of everyone involved in the education of our children. This, then, is the topic I turn to in the next chapter.

Tools for Thought from Chapter 4

Chris and Will, featured in Chapter 3, are both early career teachers; when they began teaching at Central High School, the curriculum and assessment initiatives that undergird the work described throughout this book were already starting or in place. In contrast, Gary, Kathy, and Nikki had well-established teacher identities and classroom practices that oftentimes required some negotiation with new understandings, beliefs, and expectations about student learning. Their experience is a significant reason for their effectiveness as educators, not because of their belief that they "have everything down," but because they can say with confidence that they have room to grow as well as the expertise on which to build.

In this chapter, the teachers utilized tools such as the following to initiate or support their growth through assessment:

- A student versus unit content chart to identify class-level strengths and weaknesses and to target support

- A student self-assessment chart that outlines desired behaviors and offers students a chance to record when they are engaging in those behaviors

- Full-class response to errors, knowing that mistakes are a natural part of development and should be treated as fuel for instruction rather than opportunities for punishment

Consider a time when information gathered from an assessment stared you down, asking you to consider seriously whether your practice was the most effective you could be providing students. What did you do? What factors beyond your practice did you examine? Whom did you enlist for help? Because assessment information can uncover needs much greater than those traditionally addressed in a classroom, the next chapter helps you consider the shared responsibility for responding to what we learn about students.

Chapter Five

Improving Assessment through Caring, Collaboration, and Collective Responsibility

L et's talk about assessment!" is not exactly a teacher's typical conversation starter. Suffice it to say that over the course of writing this book, when I shared its focus with friends and colleagues, I got responses that ranged from surprise to confusion to sympathy—and usually some combination thereof. The SARW help us understand why there is so much discomfort in talking about assessment in schools by reminding us that language itself

> does not contain meaning; rather, meaning is constructed in the social relationships within which language is used. Individuals make sense of language within their social relationships, their personal histories, and their collective memory. In order to make sense of even a single word, people take into account the situation and their relationship with the speaker or writer. (p. 3)

Let's consider that single word—*assessment*—and the associations it has accumulated within our profession over the past several decades. I don't think I'm being overly negative when I say that assessment, as it comes up in contemporary conversations about education, is largely synonymous with *accountability*, equating to a means by which to deny students opportunities, vilify educators, and frighten administrators into behaving in ways that are in no one's best interest except, in a very limited sense, their own. These negative associations are perhaps part of the reason why excellent teachers who, in fact, assess all the time claim not to assess at all (Genishi & Dyson, 2009).

Things don't, of course, have to be this way. The stakeholders in public education—students, families, teachers, administrators, policymakers, and the public—have, through varying degrees of activity and passivity, caused or allowed the equation of assessment with accountability to happen. It's important for us to accept the shared responsibility for letting assessment accumulate so much unproductive negativity and fear, for once we consider our complicity in this definition, we can empower ourselves to begin *living* a different one. Doing so is, in my view, the most powerful way to effect change in the broader conversation, or at least to tolerate the dissonance between a more humane definition of assessment and the dominant, oppressive one. The alternative approach to talking about assessment I'd like to offer is assessment as a form of *caring*.

Consider the simple real-life assessment question "How are you?" that we ask or are asked dozens of times a day. Luckily, this inquiry almost never has the stigma of accountability attached to it when asked in day-to-day social conversation, but we do know that it can be asked and answered in two distinct ways. The first is the way we ask it to most colleagues when we see them in the hall in the morning or between classes. It's pro forma, little more than a programmed part of our society's greeting script. The audience of the question typically understands our more or less uninvested attention, and with rare exception he or she responds with a one-word answer and life goes on. This is, I think, comparable to a view of assessment as mere formality—something that simply has to be done because it's always been done, but it isn't assessment as a sign of care.

In contrast, when I ask my son, "How are you?," I mean the question differently. I actually want to know the answer. I ask follow-up questions when I get the "Fine" accompanied by a quick glance up from his handheld video game or deck of character cards, and I make it clear that I'm interested in responding to the information he gives up, whether it's good or bad. *He* knows that it's socially acceptable to answer the question as if it were mere formality, but my job as parent is to press further, using the question to embody caring.

What if we collectively attempt to refocus our attention on and conversation around assessment not as a tool to measure, sort, and reward or punish ourselves and one another (it's always punishment in this paradigm, even if it seems there's a reward), but to demonstrate that we care about the kids in our charge and therefore seek to know more about them? And then to do the work we need to do once we learn what we learn? The SARW tell us that "different members of the school community have different but interacting interests, roles, and responsibilities" and suggest that "assessment is the medium that allows all to explore what they have learned and whether they have met their responsibilities to the school community" (p. 3). This talk of "responsibility" still sounds a bit too detached and dispassionate. What if we ignore, if only briefly and hypothetically, the SARW's attention to the differences among these stakeholders and presume that the interest they have in common is truly *caring* about the young adults whose literacy development lies not entirely, but significantly, with us?

We're All in This Together: Assessing Stakeholder Participation in Literacy Assessment

The SARW propose a lofty goal for increased involvement in literacy assessment, calling for "all stakeholders in the educational community—students, families, teachers, administrators, policymakers, and the public—[to] have an equal voice in the development, interpretation, and reporting of assessment information" (p. 28). This goal summons up in me the sentiment expressed exceedingly well by the lyrics of Stephen Sondheim, whose character Charley Cringas asks with strained resignation: "Well, what's the point of demands you *can* meet?" The standard does seem essentially an "unmeetable" demand, considering the diverse points of view the general categories of stakeholders would bring to a conversation—about what reading is, how it might be measured or described, and what to do with that information—let alone the specific interests the actual people representing those categories would hold. Just thinking about what an individual classroom teacher can do to begin effecting some of this change can be daunting.

Still, the sentiment behind this goal is one we should think about carefully. And perhaps what we'll come to realize is that as with any worthwhile endeavor with real and significant human stakes attached to it, the value of this standard lies in *improving* the way we talk about, enact, and respond to adolescent reading assessment, not actual attainment of the ideal of the standard. The SARW do go on to offer a compelling reason to seek a broader range of participation in the assessment process, noting that when one party—or even a few parties—has the upper hand in designing, interpreting, and reporting assessments, the likely result is for the disenfranchised parties to reject the value and credibility of the assessment procedure. At the same time, there is a breakdown in the relationships between those controlling the assessment and those who feel controlled by it. By contrast, the more ownership the various participants feel in the assessment process, the more seriously they value their own and others' stake in the process and *the greater the possibility of quality assessment.* (p. 29, emphasis added)

While there is value in "unloading" our negative memories and associations with assessment, in theory and in practice, I hope you're convinced by now that there is hope for teachers to reclaim an active professional role in reading assessment. This might be an appropriate time to think about an experience in which multiple stakeholders in your school or district had positive conversations about assessment, or worked together to build or improve an assessment and response system. Who was involved? What made the experience a good one, in your view?

Recall that in Chapters 1 and 2 I shared instances in which an imbalance in engagement around reading assessment resulted in the very divisiveness and dismissal the SARW mention here; I'm sure you can think of examples from your own experiences as well. This chapter, then, offers insights about how to bring us closer to the ideal of collaboration the SARW call for, culled both from the practical experiences I've had in focusing on reading assessment over the last few years and from an informed theoretical perspective.

If you are interested in beginning the serious work of improving the level of engagement around, and therefore quality of, adolescent reading assessment beyond the level of the individual classroom, an excellent starting point would be to preassess how much the various groups mentioned in Standard 10 (SARW, p. 28) are involved in the assessment process at your school. Teachers, administrators, and other interested individuals might use a chart such as the one in Figure 5.1 to describe the quality and quantity of involvement of each of the stakeholder groups in the assessment process. My experience tells me that most schools or districts, like mine, will be able to locate immediately groups that are more highly involved in all three of the assessment processes (likely policymakers, administrators, teachers—perhaps in that order) and three groups that are less, or not at all, involved in assessment (likely the public, families, and students). This estimate is an overgeneralization, of course, but it does get at the value of such a "taking stock" activity: there will be clear areas of great need that seem extremely challenging (how, for example, do we engage families meaningfully in the development of reading assessment?) and areas in which progress seems perhaps more attainable (how do we improve students' ability and desire to take up or interpret assessment information?).

Any of those three areas, and the questions they generate through discussion, is a legitimate point of inquiry that can bring school communities closer to the

Figure 5.1: How involved are the stakeholders in your community in these key aspects of reading assessment?

	Development of reading assessments (including answering the question: *What counts as reading?*)	Interpretation of reading assessments	Reporting of reading assessment information/results
Students			
Families			
Teachers			
Administrators			
Policymakers			
Public			

ideal of the SARW. The opportunity to talk about assessment in this manner—with a focus on generating possible ways for new stakeholders to be involved in the process—is certainly one way to challenge and broaden educators' notions of what assessment is and can be. The sections that follow suggest ways for doing so. Specifically, I offer examples of improved communication between teachers and administrators, a model for teacher inquiry into assessment, a suggestion for involving families in rethinking what literacy means in our schools, and a portrait of improved communication about assessment with students and parents. All of these examples are steeped in my sense of professional responsibility to care about assessment, but, more important, they are reflections of assessment done because we care about the students with whom we work.

The scale of such inquiry questions that derive from assessing stakeholder investment in assessment will vary significantly. The scope of the question you eventually choose to pursue is, in some ways, less important than your confidence in the quality of the probable conversations about reading assessment that stem from the inquiry, whatever question you choose. That said, I see a certain wisdom in purposefully selecting a pair of questions: one with a scale that is school based and implementable within the classroom setting and one that is more long term in nature and community-based in scope. Meeting unmeetable demands calls for both the courage to aim high and the good sense to start small.

Though the chart in Figure 5.1 has potential as a conversation starter for a collaborative group interested in improving multiple stakeholders in assessment, there's certainly no reason why the individual teacher wouldn't be an appropriate starting point instead. Consider using this chart as a tool for reflection on questions such as:

- How involved are students in my assessment practices, beyond taking the assessments?

- What kinds of communication occur with other teachers about the kinds of assessments I'm using?

- How often, if ever, have I communicated my views on assessment to politicians or policymakers? (The Take Action page on the NCTE website www.ncte.org/action offers ways to do so.)

Teachers and Administrators Developing Shared Understandings of High-Stakes Tests

An effective starting point for cross-stakeholder conversations in my district came from a group of teachers and administrators taking a close look together at the reading assessment that has the most political and, therefore, curricular clout in our state: the ACT Reading Test. Luckily for us, the ACT engages in a great deal of research on itself. As we culled through report after report aimed at convincing us of the test's reliability, validity, and value as a means of helping teachers know how to teach their students more effectively, we stumbled upon a section from their 2006 report, *Reading between the Lines: What the ACT Reveals about College Readiness in Reading* (available at www.act.org/research/policymakers/pdf/reading_report.pdf), which offered a new way of thinking about the test, verifying teachers' claims that the test could do little to inform their day-to-day instruction.

In the section "Ready or Not: What Matters in Reading," the authors of the report effectively nullify the all-too-common approach of trying to squeeze formative assessment information out of the ACT (e.g., Are students better at answering literal questions or inferential questions? Are they better at questions about main ideas, comparing characters, or interpreting sequences of events?) by sharing data that suggest that students at each of the score levels answer literal and inferential questions at about the same rate. In other words, students at the lower levels do poorly at both literal and inferential questions; students at the higher levels do well at both. The same is true for the different question types such as vocabulary, main idea, and cause and effect: students who get similar overall scores answer those different kinds of questions at roughly the same rate. The focus or level of inference the question requires doesn't matter; all that matters, the authors of the report reveal, is text complexity.

As a school-based reading assessment, then, the ACT Reading Test offers teachers only one piece of information: the answer to the question, "On the day the student took the test, could he or she rapidly and independently read text that is as challenging as the text on the assessment?" If the score is in the 21 range, the answer is "probably." If the score is in the 12 range, the answer is "almost certainly not." Seeking and assuming information about students' abilities beyond that is, by the ACT's own admission, futile.

Teachers at my school with sections of English populated almost exclusively with students whose scores hover in the low to mid teens, then, could no longer be asked in good conscience, "What are you doing with the information from the state reading test?," because their instruction was tied to a specific curriculum that offered few reading selections that respected their own carefully gathered assessment information about students' ability to access complex text. This realization—simultaneously a watershed and completely commonsensical—led to a yearlong curriculum revision for two English courses that involved construction of units built around themes, not specific texts, to allow for differentiation in the books students read. This is not to say that these students with lower scores on the ACT Reading assessment will never read challenging, traditional "college-preparatory" texts. But it is unreasonable to think that they will make developmental gains if all they are given to read is text that we know is beyond their level of independent access.

The discovery and sharing of this information, ensuing conversations (some of them uncomfortable because they required us all to reflect on past practice that didn't mirror a truly caring approach to assessment), and resultant action would not have been possible without the existence of a forum that semimonthly brings together teachers, building-level administrators, and district administrators to discuss issues of curriculum, instruction, and assessment (ours has taken on the unfortunate acronym of CIA, so I suggest you choose a name that doesn't abbreviate to something that implies secrecy or intelligence). Such a convergence of stakeholders, where the insights of classroom teachers are valued just as much as those of assistant superintendents, is crucial if schools are to move past the myths and misconceptions of reading assessment to the much more

Our cross-stakeholder Curriculum-Instruction-Assessment Committee is both an example of and a vehicle for meeting the SARW's call for "administrators [to] ask themselves hard questions about whether the structures they have established support staff development, teacher reflection, and student learning" (p. 3). At these meetings, our assistant superintendent asks us to look at one or two initiatives, the current information or data we have about their implementation and impact on student achievement, and potential responses to it. My favorite aspect of these meetings is the professional freedom to question and challenge the data in front of us—what they are purported to represent, who constructed the data and how, and whether there might be other, perhaps better sources of information we could use to assess and respond to curriculum, instruction, and assessment. Ultimately, these collaborations assist administrators because "those [who are] responsible for requiring an assessment are responsible for demonstrating how these assessment practices benefit and do not harm individual students" (SARW, p. 12).

challenging truths. I consider myself extremely fortunate to work in a district with key administrators who see the value in gathering multiple levels of stakeholders to explore and discuss such issues around curriculum, instruction, and assessment.

Not everyone has the luxury of working in this kind of setting, however, so I suggest that the impetus for forming such a collaborative might come from a group of teachers taking their learning from a semester-long inquiry around reading assessment to a building administrator. In my experience, principals and other administrators are much more receptive to hearing about the beginning of a solution to a problem or a question than they are to hearing only about the problem or question itself.

Once a politically powerful standardized reading assessment is unseated as the primary source of information about students as readers, as it was in our case, the information vacuum opens up, to be populated by the work of teachers engaging in collaborative assessment and analysis of student work such as that illustrated in Chapters 2, 3, and 4. Our high schools have built into their workday schedules time for collaboration—not enough, but more than in many places and certainly more than we ourselves had five years ago—during which these kinds of conversations can take place. Without such time, asking teachers to pursue this work is unethical. With proper support in terms of time, resources, and professional development, the SARW's call for the teacher to be "the most important agent of assessment" (p. 13) can be an empowering badge of honor; without such support, it is an empty proclamation that will no doubt generate resentment and no gains in student achievement.

Teacher Groups Collaborating about Reading Assessment

The kinds of conversations I have described about principled reading assessment that can and must take place after politically powerful assessments are recognized for what they are and are not can be fraught with both peril and possibility. Recognizing the limitations of available data is the natural beginning of inquiry. "Here's what we know" is the start of such a conversation. Then, "Here's what our curriculum asks our students to do. What do we need to know about our students in order to start on the path toward that accomplishment?"

More often than not, though, teachers don't have an immediate sense of what information they need beyond what a standardized test can tell them, and too often the instructional responses that assessment information may imply are not within a teacher's control. I recall one instance several years ago in which a teacher in our English department administered the Gates-MacGinitie reading test to a grade 9 honors English class and discovered that only a few students read above the fifth-grade level. She had planned to begin a full-class study of *A Tale of Two Cities* the next day. This teacher found herself in a situation nearly as paradoxical as the novel's oft-quoted first line. It was perhaps useful to know that students were not reading at the level she expected for this age and this course, but with a rigid curriculum that let specific titles determine course rigor, tension and frustration were the result. Certainly students *can* do more than a single-shot assessment suggests they can do, but it's also true that when a group's data are as consistent and compelling as hers were, the study of a Dickens novel is not the greatest place to expect discovery and development of reading strengths.

This unfortunate example reminds us that response to assessment information has to be in the back of teachers' minds even before they administer an assessment, which can be a tall order in some circumstances. High schools were not, after all, designed for flexibility. Teachers therefore need to be afforded the professional dignity of seeing their exploration of formative reading assessment as low-stakes, context-specific inquiry. Giving teachers the time, space, and resources for such inquiry-centered conversations is central to changing the way teachers see themselves as assessors, how they communicate about and enact assessment, and how curriculum, instruction, and assessment can support rather than compete with one another.

The popular and political rhetoric calling for "results now" and demanding immediate changes in teacher practice and student performance, based neither on sound research nor any school's lived reality, runs counter to this recommendation for low-stakes, deep inquiry. In the face of such pleas for rapid change, I always have to ask, "How has that approach worked so far?" I certainly understand the urgency of improving practice with diligence and passion—we're talking about students who do not get to do high school again, in contrast to our opportunity to refine our practice over many years. But to ignore the realities of adult learning, human development, and institutional inertia is simply foolish.

For all their limitations, I see the Common Core State Standards (CCSS) as a potential starting point for such inquiry into what it means to read and how teachers can best assess and support reading development. Though I realize the CCSS may at this point be a "movement" some teachers are attempting to live through or work actively against—both completely understandable stances—they offer a framework for defining reading that includes important attention to the issues of text complexity and reading in digital spaces that many previous standards have overlooked. Careful study of the CCSS regarding literacy in multiple content areas, along with the generation of a list of processes that we know from our own experience readers use as they interact with text, can help teachers begin to construct their own understanding of reading—and to look for clues in the annotations students make (as in Chapter 2) and the work they produce (as in Chapters 3 and 4). When I was first experimenting with this form of assessment, I read a student's annotations on a semester exam and attempted to describe his work on one of the charts I shared in Chapter 2 (Figure 2.8). A math teacher who shares office space with me asked what I was doing, and I explained that I was trying to grade semester exams. He commented that it looked more like I was collecting research data. Granted, the activities involved in grading a test and collecting data can resemble each other, but this comment made me realize that my approach was substantially different from the way I had assessed work in the past.

Assessing this way was more mentally taxing, less precise, and, in my view, a lot more fun. But because not everyone will respond as enthusiastically as I did to such a shift, it is advisable to start small. Supportive groups of teachers, either of

---

The SARW make two key assertions about teacher development in the realm of assessment as it relates to student learning:

- "The foundation of [effective formative literacy] assessment . . . is deep and diverse knowledge of individual students and of reading and writing" (p. 15).

- "If teachers are able to make informed assessments and articulate them well, it is largely because they have been engaged in dialogue about their students' reading, writing, and learning and have been supported by the larger community in doing so" (p. 26).

Because most of us teach too many students and often do not have formal backgrounds in literacy learning, I suggest the following guidelines for beginning and supporting teacher inquiry into their literacy assessment practices:

Begin learning about reading *through* and *with* your students by choosing some professional literature from the annotated bibliography and reading it while you examine student annotations. How do you see their work reflecting and extending the definitions and conceptions of reading from the professional literature? From the Common Core State Standards?

Choose a mode of response that you will use as a teacher to begin effecting change in your students' habits and skills as readers. This might be an approach you cull from the professional readings or a response you adapt from earlier chapters of this book. Might you use think-alouds, as Chris and Will did? Might you create a key skill/concept chart, as Gary did, and use it to focus your in-class help with certain students?

Don't go this alone! Whether or not your school-day structure supports such collaboration, find a way to work with one or more like-minded teachers, ideally someone from your discipline (department) or someone with whom you have students in common (team). When possible, share your learning, frustrations, and professional needs with administrators. The SARW remind us that "contrasting perspectives," usually available only when we work together to examine multiple forms of student work, "will lead not only to a more productive understanding of the specific student's development but also to an enhanced awareness of possible interpretations of other students' development—and of what it means to develop" (p. 25)

the same course or in cross-disciplinary teams, can look at work from one or two students over the course of a quarter or semester, developing both a sense of what adolescent reading comprehension is and how one or a few of their students read and respond to text in a range of contexts. With the support of colleagues engaged in the same kind of inquiry-based assessment (as exemplified in Chapter 2), the work this requires, from construction of new tools that offer the information teachers need to improve learning to the consequent changes in curriculum and instruction the information implies, can be viewed as the empowering activity described by the SARW.

Bringing Families into the Assessment Conversation through Online Reading

Thus far, this book has focused exclusively on reading and responding to alphabetic text on the static printed page, the kind of reading schools have traditionally privileged and will likely continue to privilege for some time. If we were to ask our students and their families, however, how they access most of what they read outside of school, we would find a great deal of it is digital text: multimedia webpages accessed through the Internet. Though we often ask students to use information from Web-based sources—selecting search terms and sorting through search results; selecting and following links; comprehending the words, images, sound, and video on the pages—we typically don't assess students' ability to do all of these things formatively, in the moment as they happen, but instead summatively and from too great a distance, when a final paper or project is submitted.

Because policymakers, at the present moment the most powerful stakeholders in the assessment process, have not yet captured the assessment space for digital reading, there is a natural opportunity for schools and families to work together to develop a vision for local assessment of online reading. Even when large-scale assessment of how students read online does occur, it cannot possibly match the authenticity and flexibility of the kind of assessment that can happen within a classroom when teachers and others can informally observe learners in the process of finding and comprehending information. Unlike print text, the Web and how we read it will change over time in ways that will require the assessment of such processes to be nimble and flexible. Involving parents as partners in this way, bringing them into the fold of inquiring into what it means for their children to be literate and how we can best work together to support those developing literacies, embodies assessment as a form of caring. At the same time, it heeds the SARW's call to "engage parents and the local community in conversations about the goals they have for the ways children will use reading and writing and the ways reading and writing are [actually] used in the community" (p. 27).

Leu and colleagues (2007) and Coiro and Dobler (2007) offer us compelling reasons to believe that reading online is different enough from reading traditional print to merit new kinds of inquiry into literacy in digital environments. They suggest that reading online differs in at least these key ways:

- The prior knowledge of search engines to locate information
- The higher degree of forward inferential reasoning required by readers
- The rapid nature of self-regulation, including physical regulation of mouse and keyboard coordination

Because most schools do not yet have an assessment tool for online reading, family members could be invited in to the school setting to help construct a vision for what online reading is and how it might be assessed. We would not, I hope, attempt to engage our families by asking them to take a standardized reading test, but if we pose to families a research question such as "How does school funding impact student achievement?," ask them to search for the answers, and then discuss the skills, actions, and dispositions required to confirm and disconfirm information, then we've come a long way toward enfranchising the family as a stakeholder in what literacy means and how we might assess it.

Families also could get involved in developing and refining a preassessment tool such as Figure 5.2, which I've used in classes to determine which areas of online reading need the most attention through full-class focus lessons and think-aloud demonstrations. Further, because schools typically lack the recording software that researchers use to assess students' online reading habits (see, for example, Coiro, 2009), family and community members could be recruited to serve as additional kid-watchers and questioners. For example, despite my well-intentioned instruction on the need to look carefully at domain names to assess a site's suitability, my student and I would have benefited from an extra pair of eyes when he wasted a lot of time using a "co.uk" site—a site with content pertinent to Great Britain—to answer questions about how he might obtain a summer job in our Illinois town. The Internet, as they say, has everything, and helping students understand how to navigate it is a job that never ends. Web-savvy parents and family members are ideal partners for in-the-moment formative assessment of online reading. Using the preassessment developed with families, community volunteers could join with teachers in kid-watching during Internet search sessions, looking for patterns of behavior that need to be addressed through instruction and prompting students to try different approaches or challenge their thinking in the moment.

Figure 5.2: An online reading preassessment.

What kinds of things do you read online?

When searching for information online, how do you typically start?

When you get a list of search results through a search engine, how do you decide which links to click and which to ignore?

When you find a site that has information that relates to your question or search, how do you decide if the information is valid and reliable? Comment on each of these features:

- The web address of the page or site
- The author(s) of the site
- The layout or appearance of the site
- The purpose or agenda of the site

When you're reading about a topic that is familiar to you, what do you do when you read something that seems new, surprising, or contradictory to what you already know?

Students as Participants in Their Own Assessment Process

Perhaps the most important information students can get about themselves as readers is genuine feedback from teachers—feedback that comes in just the right moment and with the immediate opportunity to apply it. Sometimes students create written products that reveal their understanding through reading, and these products can then be the focus of written or verbal feedback from their teachers. I've found a much more productive and immediate feedback loop, however, in individual reading conferences, each requiring ten minutes, the student, a text he or she has selected to read, and the teacher. Reading conferences are certainly no new invention, but the first time I conducted one as a high school teacher, I was nervous. No one had shown me how to run one, all the reading I had done on the topic was based in an elementary context, and I had no idea what I'd say when a student talked with me about what he or she was reading. More unnervingly, I had no idea how the students would respond.

My first round of reading conferences, then, involved *me* talking very little. After a few weeks of fairly strictly enforced quiet reading time with their independent reading choices (I knew that conferring with one student while the rest of the class fell apart was a trap I didn't want to get caught in), I went around the room with a yellow legal pad, writing the student's name down before I approached him or her, and then said one thing: "Tell me about what you're reading." For the rest of the three- or four-minute conference, I listened. And I wrote. I knew I didn't yet have the capacity to respond to student information in the moment, but I was confident that if I paid careful enough attention, I'd be able to look over those notes, in combination with other assessment information I had, and eventually figure out what to do.

Taking this risk as a teacher—moving from mere manager of sustained silent reading to gatherer of the most personalized assessment information I've ever collected—has been one of the great rewards of my career. First of all, the genuine follow-up questions I asked my students about plot and characters validated what they were doing, as did the sincere "Thank you for talking with me" with which I ended each conference. Second, it helped me pinpoint the questions I knew I needed to dig a little deeper into—again, inquiry is about the right questions, not the easy answers. Third, it normalized the idea of one-on-one feedback. Our secondary schools are designed in such a way that a student typically gets individualized attention from an adult only if something bad happens: a detention resulting from a discipline infraction, after-school help when a grade slips. Making it natural for the student and teacher to collaborate on assessment goes a long way toward reframing assessment as inquiry rather than punishment or mere procedure.

From these informal reading conferences, which eventually enabled me to ask much more focused questions after I had jotted a few sessions worth of notes, I was able to establish the routine of portfolio conferences. My students collected a range of work in their portfolios. Then, while most of the class read or completed work that didn't require my immediate intervention, I would call one or two students each period over to a side table and ask something like, "Here's a list of the kinds of things we know effective readers do while they're reading. Can you share with me some work that shows me this is something you can do well?"

At first, this approach tends to make students uncomfortable; although the act of assessment has its etymological root of "sitting beside," our formal practices in school have transformed assessment into a fairly impersonal transaction. The immediacy of talk, as opposed to written feedback that is so readily ignored or discarded despite our valiant hours spent providing it, has a potent effect. I recall vividly a portfolio conference with Charisse, a student I hadn't yet "figured out." When I called on her in full-class discussion, Charisse relied on her seemingly reflexive response of a shoulder shrug, followed by a defiant, "I told you I don't know" when I probed a step further. In the conference, I asked her which of our course goals she thought she had the least facility with. As I asked, I was repeating rapidly

An undercurrent of this section is the amount of time my students spent reading as an independent or collaborative instructional activity. Though there is merit in simply giving students time to read in class, doing so is absolutely essential if teachers are going to get to know their students as readers. Again, this makes so much sense, but the institutional tradition of seeing reading as homework and class time as the site of discussion or recitation gets in the way. The SARW support independent and collaborative reading, pointing out that "the reliability of interpretations of assessment data is likely to improve when there are multiple opportunities to observe reading and writing. . . . [S]ampling more than one aspect of literacy permits a closer approximation of the complexity of reading, writing, listening, and speaking processes as they occur and as they are used in real-life settings" (p. 25).

in my head, "*Make high- and low-level inferences from information the author gives you.*" To my amazement, that's precisely what she said, as she pointed to the words on the page of the goal sheet.

Charisse claimed she could find no evidence of her ability to infer from context in her portfolio, so I asked her to get her independent reading book so we could read together for a while. We took turns reading a passage from Sapphire's *Push* in which a character meets with a receptionist at a social service agency. When I asked Charisse to tell me about the receptionist, one of the first things she told me was that the woman was black. I asked Charisse how in the world she knew that, and she pointed out—as if I were an idiot—the description of the receptionist's hairstyle and the manner in which she interacted with the main character. I'd never felt like a smarter idiot!

Charisse knew what had happened too. We had identified something she wasn't sure she could do, engaged in the task that would allow it to happen, and, finally, we reflected on the way Charisse's effort and prior knowledge made it happen. Sure, the conference took considerable time away from what might be considered traditional instruction in a high school setting, and no, I didn't get to meet with every student as often as I would have liked. But for the students for whom my more efficient modes of assessment were not effective, nothing I did was more valuable than the personal conference.

So, while I cannot claim expertise as a conferrer, I can offer these suggestions from the literature and my own practice of reading conferences:

- **If you can, start the conference with a specific purpose.** This is difficult to do at the beginning of conference cycles, but once you get things going, the conferences direct themselves. At the end of every conference, I ask the student, "What should we talk about next time?" Oftentimes I get a shrug and awkward silence, so I offer options such as making a prediction to discuss or confirm, asking a question that the student hopes to address in the upcoming reading, or looking for a sentence or two that the student thinks is really good writing.

- **If you're just getting started, prepare some questions in advance.** "What's going on in this part of the book?" "Who's your main character and what is he or she like?" Just a few of these conversation starters affixed to your clipboard can give you a place to start.

- **Don't be afraid to ask the student to read to you.** As we saw in Stephanie Royse's class in Chapter 2, we can learn a lot from asking students to read and think aloud. Have the student share what's going on in the story and then read a paragraph or two. Ask him or her to share observations about what's going on and what's making sense in the reading.

- **Let the student do the talking.** The more you listen, the more students will tell you about what and how they're reading. Jot everything down, and if an insight comes to you while you're chatting with a student, write it down immediately. The time spent taking that analytic note is better than the frustration of not being able to remember your discovery when it's time to plan.

A Dream Reframed: Discussing Reading Achievement with Families

A natural extension of my portfolio conversations was, of course, an ability to engage in a knowledgeable conversation with families about their child's development as a reader in my classroom. The SARW frame this responsibility as being able to "help families and community members understand the assessment process and the range of tools that can be useful in painting a detailed picture of learning" (p. 27). Remember that third dream from Chapter 1, the one with the grade sheet, inquisitive parent, and shrieking violins? Hokey, I know, but I needed to construct such a scenario to work against as I set for myself the goal of developing the ability to conduct parent conferences that not only allow for such questioning but also are specifically designed around the tough questions of student development as readers.

In one particularly satisfying parent–teacher conference (one in which the student was present, which has its advantages and drawbacks), Brian, his mom, and I were able to look through Brian's work folder at his course preassessment and his work on several subsequent reading assessments. We could all see the development in his response to text, in both quantity and quality, as well as improved command over his thinking, as evidenced by asking questions that he clearly sought the answers to as he continued reading. In that regard, the conference was positive.

I had to share, however, my finding that Brian had demonstrated no growth from his eighth-grade EXPLORE Reading Test to the one I administered midyear. Almost every other student had demonstrated about two points of growth—double what would be expected, if we believe the information the ACT produces about itself. Both Brian and his mom agreed that this was cause for some concern, and I admitted that I didn't know why his class work showed such a change while his performance on a standardized measure did not.

We agreed to the following plan of inquiry: I would find a teacher who would allow me to "borrow" Brian for one period so that I could administer the Adolescent Literacy Inventory (ALI) (Brozo & Afflerbach, 2011), a comprehensive interactive assessment tool that allows students to read and respond to text from grade-level content textbooks. I would share any insights from that assessment, and we would then consider ways to change instruction in light of what we learned.

The SARW remind us that

> formal tests need to be considerably more complex than is generally true today. Tests that accommodate multiple responses, different types of texts and tasks, and indicators of attitude and motivation are all essential to a comprehensive view of literacy achievement. Whenever possible, assessments must specify the types of tests, tasks, and situations used for assessment purposes and note whether and when students' performance was improved by variations in text quality, type or task, or situation. (p. 19)

The Adolescent Literacy Inventory (Brozo & Afflerbach, 2011) was specifically designed to meet such high standards. Students complete content area MAZE passages to help teachers determine an appropriate level of text complexity for further assessment. Then students and teachers read and discuss content area texts together, allowing teachers to see how students process text and how they respond to modeling or suggestions from the administering teacher. I take copious notes during an administration of the ALI. As soon as possible after the assessment, I write up a detailed description of the student's performance, concluding with observations, insights, recommendations, and limitations of the assessment event. I've learned an incredible amount about my most enigmatic learners through this tool and its administration process.

At the time, I had the good fortune of hosting a university intern who was working toward his reading endorsement, and the two of us assessed Brian with the ALI. Amidst Brian's many strengths, including the ability to summon up topical and word-specific background knowledge and demonstrate understanding of grade-level text through embedded and end-of passage questions, Brian demonstrated marked difficulty with fluency, the ability to pronounce words rapidly and string them together naturally and with little effort. Rasinski et al. (2005) remind us of the significant role that lack of fluency can play in hindering adolescent reading achievement, even though it's largely considered a skill that is "learned" in the lower grades. We saw that Brian often ignored punctuation, miscalled words based on their first few letters, and paused frequently, but never to patch up comprehension based on any of these errors.

After consultation with his mother, I had Brian meet with the university intern for a dozen or so one-on-one tutoring sessions, both over his lunch period and during independent reading time in my class. Brian selected a book from a list of titles I thought would interest him based on information I'd gathered from past conferences, and he and the intern took turns reading aloud and discussing Chris Crutcher's *Running Loose*. At first, the intern would read a paragraph fluently and ask Brian to read back the same paragraph in the same way. Over time, as the intern monitored the frequency of errors vis-à-vis Brian's comprehension, he let Brian do the reading on his own. As with any intervention, we can't be certain of the effect it had specifically on Brian's achievement, but both he and his mom were pleased to learn that on the spring administration of the PLAN Reading Test (actually designed for sophomores), Brian demonstrated four points of growth from his eighth-grade assessment, more than twice the expected gain.

Brian's case is in some ways exceptional in the sense that the roadblock to his comprehension was obvious to us once we found the right tool to help us uncover it; his interpersonal connection with the university mentor also undoubtedly contributed to the enthusiasm with which this ninth grader took to giving up lunch to work on improving reading fluency. That aside, the pride all of us—student, parent, preservice teacher, and teacher—were able to take in working together to gather and interpret assessment information speaks to the value of heeding the call of the SARW to make literacy assessment a focal point of cross-stakeholder conversations.

Conclusions

These scenarios only begin to address the challenge to ensure that "all those inquiring into the nature and effectiveness of educational practices are responsible for investigating the roles they have played" (SARW, p. 3). The complicated intersection of national, state, and local contexts that define any one school make it impossible to offer blanket recommendations regarding paths toward achieving the goal of bringing multiple, diverse stakeholders into meaningful conversation about reading assessment.

The SARW do, however, make the tenuous assertion that "when administrators, families, and the public become involved together in assessment issues, trusting relationships are likely to evolve" (p. 27). I may be overly skeptical in my reading of that sentence, but given the accountability context surrounding literacy assessment in our schools today, I see a *potential* for trusting relationships to evolve, but not necessarily a *likelihood*. I can imagine such conversations, handled poorly, leading—by design or by accident—to finger-pointing and self-interested blaming. Handled well and filtered through a philosophy of care for our students as learners, citizens, and human beings, not out of blasé necessity or political accountability, conversations about assessment might build trust. But even then, the histories schools have of meting out rewards based on literacy assessment, coupled with teachers' inability to develop new bodies of expertise and instructional response at the request of a committee, complicate the situation.

For the foreseeable future, the Common Core State Standards, with their rallying cry of "Fewer, higher, clearer," will likely play a part in any such conversations. A crucial component of these conversations, about both the standards themselves and how we should assess our students' development toward them, is the understanding that "the commonly expressed need for 'higher standards' is better expressed as the need for higher quality instruction, for without it, higher standards simply means denying greater numbers of students access to programs and opportunities" (SARW, p. 16). A set of learning standards as part of a curriculum document holds little promise on its own for the improvement of the literate lives of our students. Supporting teachers engaged in inquiry-based, classroom-specific assessments—because they care, not just because they're told to—is the unavoidably challenging route toward making the rewards of that higher-quality instruction a reality.

Annotated Bibliography

Understanding Reading Comprehension and Suggestions on How to Teach It

Appleman, Deborah
Adolescent Literacy and the Teaching of Reading: Lessons for Teachers of Literature.
Urbana, IL: NCTE, 2010. Print.

If we assess it, we're obligated to teach it. Deborah Appleman's smart and approachable text helps teachers, particularly English teachers, reenvision themselves as teachers of literature *and* teachers of reading. Her chapter on assessment offers useful tools that address readers' histories and affect, a useful complement to assessments that are more cognitive and metacognitive in nature.

Braunger, Jane, and Jan Patricia Lewis
Building a Knowledge Base in Reading. 2nd ed.
Newark, DE: IRA; Urbana, IL: NCTE, 2005. Print.

Though a much-condensed version of this book is included as a chapter in Kucer (2008), Braunger and Lewis's full discussion of the thirteen core understandings about reading and the research behind them is indispensible to teachers who seek to support their students as readers.

Daniels, Harvey, and Steve Zemelman
Subjects Matter: Every Teacher's Guide to Content-Area Reading.
Portsmouth, NH: Heinemann, 2004. Print.

If you're embarking on an inquiry into reading assessment with a group of cross-content teachers, this book offers insights into how and why we can support reading in the content areas. It also provides a number of tools to prompt thinking that produces student work that can then become the object of inquiry and assessment.

Fisher, Douglas, Nancy Frey, and Diane Lapp
In a Reading State of Mind: Brain Research, Teacher Modeling, and Comprehension Instruction.
Newark, DE: IRA, 2009. Print and DVD.

With sections on the neural and social significance of modeling, as well as on comprehension, word solving, and text structures, this smart and practical book can serve as a centerpiece for teacher inquiry into what it means to read and teach reading. The accompanying DVD with classroom examples strengthens this already useful volume.

Kucer, Stephen B., ed.
What Research Really Says about Teaching and Learning to Read.
Urbana, IL: NCTE, 2008. Print.

I cited heavily from Kucer's chapter on the dimensions of reading, but I also recommend Michael Shaw's chapter on supporting struggling readers, as well as the Decision-Making Matrix (Appendix C) for its usefulness in inquiring into reading curriculum and materials.

Lapp, Diane, and Douglas Fisher, eds.
Essential Readings on Comprehension.
Newark, DE: IRA, 2009. Print.

Fisher and Lapp compile fifteen articles from various International Reading Association journals in one convenient resource that helps teachers understand what comprehension is and how to teach it. Of particular interest is the article "'You Can Read This—I'll Show You How': Interactive Comprehension Instruction," which Lapp and Fisher cowrote with Maria Grant.

Lattimer, Heather
Reading for Learning: Using Discipline-Based Texts to Build Content Knowledge.
Urbana, IL: NCTE, 2010. Print.

Each chapter of this book contains an "Assessment *for* Learning" section that stresses the connections among learning goals, classroom practices, and assessment. Loaded with classroom examples and student work, Lattimer's discussion helps teachers bridge the gap between content learning and reading as a vehicle for such learning.

Schoenbach, Ruth, Cynthia Greenleaf, Christina Cziko, and Lori Harwitz
Reading for Understanding: A Guide to Improving Reading in Middle and High School Classrooms.
San Francisco: Jossey-Bass; Urbana, IL: NCTE, 1999. Print.

When I first began my study of reading comprehension, this book offered practical advice and a framework for using my existing expertise as a skilled comprehender of academic text as an instructional resource for bringing students into the fold of academic literacy.

Swartz, Robert J., Arthur L. Costa, Barry K. Beyer, Rebecca Reagan, and Bena Kallick
Thinking-Based Learning: Activating Students' Potential.
Norwood, MA: Christopher-Gordon, 2008. Print.

Not everything in this book relates directly to teaching reading, but conceiving comprehension as the thoughtful intersection of kids' lived experiences and the text in front of them makes it quite valuable. Chapter 6, "Assessing Skillful Thinking," offers some useful tools and stances for teachers to take as they look for evidence of their students' thinking as they read.

Wolfe, Maryanne
Proust and the Squid: The Story and Science of the Reading Brain.
New York: Harper Perennial, 2008. Print.

Who knew that the story of reading and human development could be turned into a popular page-turner? Wolfe's exploration of the biological structures that have evolved and adapted to facilitate the invention and use of written language both informs professional practice and deepens one's appreciation of the human condition.

Reading Assessment and General Books on Assessment

Afflerbach, Peter
Understanding and Using Reading Assessment K–12.
Newark, DE: IRA, 2007. Print.

Certainly among the most influential thinkers in the field of reading assessment, Afflerbach offers a book that addresses big ideas about assessment, such as validity and reliability, as well as sections on different types of assessments. Particularly interesting to secondary teachers is his chapter on performance assessment.

Dolgin, Joanna, Kim Kelly, and Sarvenaz Zelkha
Authentic Assessments for the English Classroom.
Urbana, IL: NCTE, 2010. Print.

Heavily contextualized in their work in an urban secondary school, Dolgin, Kelly, and Zehlka offer a range of formative and summative assessments as an integral part of an English curriculum. The sections on assessing independent reading are especially valuable.

Elbow, Peter
"Ranking, Evaluating, and Liking: Sorting Out Three Forms of Judgment."
College English 55.2 (1993): 187–206. Print.

This essay had an immediate effect on the way I read and assessed student writing when I read it as part of my graduate work in writing studies. Elbow's finely shaded views on different forms of assessment inform the way I look at students' development as readers as well.

Fisher, Douglas, and Nancy Frey
Checking for Understanding: Formative Assessment Techniques for Your Classroom.
Alexandria, VA: ASCD, 2007. Print.

This resource offers dozens of assessment tools and plenty of smart thinking about how and why to use them, organized around five modes of assessment: through oral language, questioning, writing, projects, and tests.

Langer, Georgea, Amy B. Colton, and Loretta S. Goff
Collaborative Analysis of Student Work: Improving Teaching and Learning.
Alexandria, VA: ASCD, 2003. Print.

"Amazing things happen when teachers analyze a student's learning over a period of months," begins this book that offers a smart and highly organized model for teachers interested in working together to examine their students' work.

Popham, W. James
Transformative Assessment.
Alexandria, VA: ASCD, 2008. Print.

Though not everything Popham discusses in this book translates to the complexity of reading comprehension, his thinking about the roles that teachers and students play in the formative assessment process—as well as his attention to the changes in classroom climate that it brings and requires—will help teachers see the "big picture" of formative assessment.

Serafini, Frank
"Three Paradigms of Assessment: Measurement, Procedure, and Inquiry."
Reading Teacher 54.4 (2000–2001): 384–93. Print.

Though published in a journal serving teachers of younger students, this essay is worth tracking down through your school or university library. Serafini's argument for inquiry-based assessment in light of an understanding of reading as an act of constructive inquiry is compelling and insightful.

Understanding the Curriculum– Instruction–Assessment Connection

Sipe, Rebecca Bowers
Adolescent Literacy at Risk? The Impact of Standards.
Urbana, IL: NCTE, 2009. Print.

As districts and states respond to and implement the Common Core State Standards, I can't imagine a more useful book to help teachers understand the value and limitations of standards. Sipe includes a chapter on how assessment and standards can work together to support student learning.

Wiggins, Grant, and Jay McTighe
Understanding by Design. 2nd ed.
Alexandria, VA: ASCD, 2005. Print.

When I came back to the classroom, reading this book prompted an incredible amount of reflection and gave language and clarity to much of my intuitive, experience-based understanding of effective teaching and learning. "Thinking like an Assessor" is a particularly germane chapter, but the book's true value is helping teachers see the interconnections between curricular clarity, focused assessment, and effective instruction.

Teacher Inquiry

Goswami, Dixie, Ceci Lewis, Marty Rutherford, and Diane Waff
On Teacher Inquiry: Approaches to Language and Literacy Research.
New York: Teachers College, 2009. Print.

This edited collection, part of the National Conference on Research in Language and Literacy series, can deepen inquiry practitioners' sense of why and how to engage in careful study of their classroom practices and the student learning that results.

Hubbard, Ruth Shagoury, and Brenda Miller Power
The Art of Classroom Inquiry: A Handbook for Teacher-Researchers. Rev. ed.
Portsmouth, NH: Heinemann, 2003. Print.

It's impossible to discuss teacher inquiry without a mention of this practical and thoughtful guide to asking questions about teaching and learning in our classrooms. A clear structure and plenty of examples make the act of teacher research seem both achievable and necessary in this nearly classic work.

Classroom Structures That Support Effective Use of Assessment

Fisher, Douglas, and Nancy Frey
Better Learning through Structured Teaching: A Framework for the Gradual Release of Responsibility.
Alexandria, VA: ASCD, 2008. Print.

The assessment-informed interconnections between modeling, guided practice, collaboration, and independent work make this instructional model key to implementing differentiated instruction with integrity.

Johnston, Peter H.
Choice Words: How Our Language Affects Children's Learning.
Portland, ME: Stenhouse, 2004. Print.

Demonstrating that all classroom interactions are mediated by language we use, particularly spoken language, Johnston offers concrete suggestions for ways of talking to encourage self-assessment and to nurture growth and development.

Serravallo, Jennifer, and Gravity Goldberg
Conferring with Readers: Supporting Each Student's Growth and Independence.
Portsmouth, NH: Heinemann, 2007. Print.

Though written for teachers of younger students, I found this book invaluable in helping me understand how I could use the time and space of my classroom to gather and respond to assessment evidence through individual conferences. The sections on classroom structures and record-keeping are particularly useful.

Involving the Families and the Community in Quality Assessment

Fleischer, Cathy
Reading and Writing and Teens: A Parent's Guide to Adolescent Literacy.
Urbana, IL: NCTE, 2010. Print.

Opening up the conversations about reading, learning, and assessment with parents and families can be challenging. This book, written specifically for those audiences, can be a valuable tool in framing those conversations. I can imagine schools using it as a model for such conversations, or as a centerpiece of a parent–teacher book study.

Price, Hugh B.
Mobilizing the Community to Help Students Succeed.
Alexandria, VA: ASCD, 2008. Print.

Every community is different, so not all of Price's suggestions will ring true for every reader, but when we look to involve families and community members in rethinking school-based assessment practices, a book such as this can spark ideas that might work in your school.

Works Cited

ACT. (2006). *Reading between the lines: What the ACT reveals about college readiness in reading*. Retrieved from http://www.act.org/research/policymakers/pdf/reading_report.pdf

Adult, 2 teens charged with beating elderly black man. (2009, August 20). *CNN*. Retrieved from http://articles.cnn.com/2009-08-20/justice/maryland.racial.attack_1_calvin-lockner-police-beating?_s=PM:CRIME

Afflerbach, P. (2004). Assessing adolescent reading. In T. L. Jetton and J. A. Dole (Eds.), *Adolescent literacy research and practice* (pp. 369–391). New York: Guilford Press.

Afflerbach, P. (2011). Assessing reading. In T. V. Rasinski (Ed.), *Rebuilding the foundation: Effective reading instruction for 21st century literacy* (pp. 293–314). Bloomington, IN: Solution Tree Press.

Brookhart, S. (2008). *How to give effective feedback to your students*. Alexandria, VA: Association for Supervision and Curriculum Development.

Brozo, W. G. (2009). Response to intervention or responsive instruction? Challenges and possibilities of response to intervention for adolescent literacy. *Journal of Adolescent and Adult Literacy, 53*(4), 277–281.

Brozo, W. G., & Afflerbach, P. P. (2011). *Adolescent literacy inventory, grades 6–12*. New York: Allyn and Bacon.

Coiro, J. (2009). Rethinking online reading assessment. *Educational Leadership, 66*(6), 59–63.

Coiro, J., & Dobler, E. (2007). Exploring the online reading comprehension strategies used by sixth-grade skilled readers to search for and locate information on the Internet. *Reading Research Quarterly, 42*(2), 214–257.

Dean, D. (2011). *What works in writing instruction: Research and practices*. Urbana, IL: National Council of Teachers of English.

Dennis, D. V. (2008). Are assessment data really driving middle school reading instruction? What we can learn from one student's experience. *Journal of Adolescent and Adult Literacy, 51*(7), 578–587.

Dennis, D. V. (2009–2010). "I'm not stupid": How assessment drives (in)appropriate reading instruction. *Journal of Adolescent and Adult Literacy, 53*(4), 283–290.

Elbow, P. (1993). Ranking, evaluating, and liking: Sorting out three forms of judgment. *College English, 55*(2), 187–206.

Fisher, D., & Frey, N. (2007). *Checking for understanding: Formative assessment techniques for your classroom*. Alexandria, VA: Association for Supervision and Curriculum Development.

Fisher, D., & Frey, N. (2008a). *Better learning through structured teaching: A framework for the gradual release of responsibility*. Alexandria, VA: Association for Supervision and Curriculum Development.

Fisher, D., & Frey, N. (2008b). What does it take to create skilled readers? Facilitating the transfer and application of literacy strategies." *Voices from the Middle, 15*(4), 16–22.

Fisher, D., & Frey, N. (2009). *Background knowledge: The missing piece of the comprehension puzzle*. Portsmouth, NH: Heinemann.

Fisher, D., & Frey, N. (2010). *Guided instruction: How to develop confident and successful learners*. Alexandria, VA: Association for Supervision and Curriculum Development.

Frey, N., Fisher, D., & Everlove, S. (2009). *Productive group work: How to engage students, build teamwork, and promote understanding*. Alexandria, VA: Association for Supervision and Curriculum Development.

Genishi, C., & Dyson, A. H. (2009). *Children, language, and literacy: Diverse learners in diverse times*. New York: Teachers College Press; Washington, DC: National Association for the Education of Young Children.

Joint Task Force on Assessment of the International Reading Association & the National Council of Teachers of English. (2010). *Standards for the assessment of reading and writing* (Rev. ed.). Urbana, IL: National Council of Teachers of English; Newark, DE: International Reading Association.

Keene, E. O., & Zimmermann, S. (1997). *Mosaic of thought: Teaching comprehension in a reader's workshop*. Portsmouth, NH: Heinemann.

Kucan, L., & Beck, I. L. (1997). Thinking aloud and reading comprehension research: Inquiry, instruction, and social interaction. *Review of Educational Research, 67*(3), 271–99.

Kucer, S. B. (1991). Authenticity as the basis for instruction. *Language Arts, 68*(7), 532–40.

Kucer, S. B. (2005). *Dimensions of literacy: A conceptual base for teaching reading and writing in school settings* (2nd ed.). Mahwah, NJ: Erlbaum.

Kucer, S. B. (2008). What we know about the nature of reading. In S. B. Kucer (Ed.), *What research really says about teaching and learning to read* (pp. 29–61). Urbana, IL: National Council of Teachers of English.

Kucer, S. B., & Silva, C. (2006). *Teaching the dimensions of literacy*. Mahwah, NJ: Erlbaum.

Leu, D. J., Zawilinski, L., Castek, J., Banerjee, M., Housand, B. C., Liu, Y., & O'Neil, M. (2007). What is new about the new literacies of online reading comprehension? In L. S. Rush, A. J. Eakle, & A. Berger (Eds.), *Secondary school literacy: What research reveals for classroom practice* (pp. 37–68). Urbana, IL: National Council of Teachers of English.

National Council of Teachers of English. (2011). Communities of practice: A policy research brief produced by the National Council of Teachers of English. Urbana, IL: Author.

Overlie, J. (2009). Creating confident, capable learners. In T. R. Guskey (Ed.), *The teacher as assessment leader* (pp. 181–201). Bloomington, IN: Solution Tree Press.

Paris, S. G. (2005). Reinterpreting the development of reading skills. *Reading Research Quarterly, 40*(2), 184–202.

Pearson, P. D., & Gallagher, M. C. (1983). The instruction of reading comprehension. *Contemporary Educational Psychology, 8*(3), 317–344.

Popham, W. J. (2008). *Transformative assessment*. Alexandria, VA: Association for Supervision and Curriculum Development.

Rasinski, T. V., Padak, N. D., McKeon, C. A., Wilfong, L. G., Friedauer, J. A., & Heim, P. (2005). Is reading fluency a key for successful high school reading? *Journal of Adolescent and Adult Literacy, 49*(1), 22–27.

Riddle Buly, M., & Valencia, S. W. (2002). Below the bar: Profiles of students who fail state reading assessments. *Educational Evaluation and Policy Analysis, 24*(3), 219–239.

Rupp, A. A., & Lesaux, N. K. (2006). Meeting expectations? An empirical investigation of a standards-based assessment of reading comprehension. *Educational Evaluation and Policy Analysis, 28*(4), 315–333.

Scott, D. B. (2008). Assessing text processing: A comparison of four methods. *Journal of Literacy Research, 40*(3), 290–316.

Serafini, F. (2000–2001). Three paradigms of assessment: Measurement, procedure, and inquiry. *The Reading Teacher, 54*(4), 384–393.

Shepard, L. A. (2000). The role of assessment in a learning culture. *Educational Researcher, 29*(7), 4–14.

Short, K., & Burke, C. (1994). *Curriculum as inquiry.* Paper presented at the fifth Whole Language Umbrella Conference, San Diego, CA.

Silvén, M., & Vauras, M. (1992). Improving reading through thinking aloud. *Learning and Instruction, 2*(2), 69–88.

Wiggins, G., & McTighe, J. (2005). *Understanding by design* (2nd ed.). Alexandria, VA: Association for Supervision and Curriculum Development.

Index

Accountability, 104
ACT, 12, 108
    lack of formative assessment in, 108
    reading skills in, 12
    research on, 108
Active thinking, connection with reading, 22
Administrators, collaboration with teachers on assessment, 108–10
Adolescent Literacy Inventory (ALI), 118–19
Afflerbach, P., 3, 19, 26, 30, 118, 124
Allridge, W., 10, 52, 69–78
    content area knowledge unit, 69–78
Anticipation guides, 94, 95
Appleman, D., 123
Assessment
    versus accountability, 104
    classroom, 7
    consequences of, xx, 19
    fairness of, xx
    families' involvement in, xxi
    formative, 7
    language of, xvi–xviii
    of language, xvi
    nature of, xi–xiii
    negative view of, 103–4
    purpose of, xviii–xix, 19
    of reading. *See* Reading assessment
    refocusing, 104–5
    rehabilitation of, 5–8
    standardized, 4
    of student engagement, 3
    student interests in, xviii
    summative, 7
    teacher development in, 112
    teacher role in, xvii
    vilification of, 5
Autonomy, maintaining, 18

Background knowledge, assessment of, 94–97
    anticipation guide for, 94, 95
Belt, C., 10, 52–68, 69, 83
    summarization unit, 54–68
Beyer, B. K., 124
Braunger, J., 123
Brozo, W., 24, 118
Burke, C., 15

Classroom-based assessment, 7, 24–26
    challenging bad ideas with, 24–26
Cognitive dimension of reading, 14
Coiro, J., 114
Collaborative learning, 66
Colton, A. B., 125
Common Core State Standards, 54, 111, 120
Consequential validity, 19, 20
Construct validity, 19, 20

Content area knowledge, developing, 69–76
Costa, A. L., 124
Crutcher, C., 119
Cueing, 62
Curriculum, reading assessment as outgrowth of, 30–32
Cziko, C., 124

Daniels, H., 123
Dean, D., 61, 69
Decker, K., 10, 82, 94–97
    assessing background knowledge unit, 94–97
Dennis, D. V., 21
Developmental dimension of reading, 15
DiCamillo, K., 26
Dietz, L., 10, 48–50
Dobler, E., 114
Dolgin, J., 124
During-reading annotations, 21–24, 40, 41, 42, 47, 49
Dyson, A. H., 30, 104

Elbow, P., 59, 83, 124
Everlove, S., 52
Explaining and modeling, 62

Families
    discussing reading achievement with, 118–20
    including in assessment through online readings, 113–15
Feedback, assessment-based, 18
First draft reading, 98–99
Fisher, D., 6, 14, 15, 52, 62, 123, 125, 126
Fleischer, C., 126
Focus lessons, 53, 59–61
Formative assessment, 6, 7
Frey, N., 6, 14, 15, 52, 62, 123, 125, 126
Friedauer, J. A., 21

Gaines, E., 96
Gallagher, M. C., 53
Garrett, G., 59
Gates-MacGinitie reading assessment, 4, 110
Genishi, C., 30, 104
Goal clarity, 5, 11–15
Goff, L. S., 125
Goldberg, G., 126
Goodall, J., 46
Goswami, D., 125
Gradual release of responsibility (GRR) model, 52–53
Greene, B., 59
Greenleaf, C., 124
Grouping students, 79
Group work, 53
Guided reading, 24, 53, 58, 61–62

Harwitz, L., 124
Heim, P., 21
Hubbard, R. S., 126

Independent tasks, 53
Inquiry-based assessment, 15–17, 19–24
    construct and consequential validity and, 19–24
Interventions, 24–25
IRA–NCTE Joint Task Force on Assessment, *Standards for the Assessment of Reading and Writing*, Revised Edition, xi–xxi

Johnston, P. H., 126

Kallick, B., 124
Keene, E. O., 2
Kelly, K., 124
Kucer, S., 12, 13, 14, 15, 24, 123

Langer, G., 125
Language
    assessment of, xvi
    of assessment, xvi–xviii
    learning of, xv–xvi
    nature of, xiii–xiv, 103
Lapp, D., 123
Lattimer, H., 123
Learning of language, xv–xvi
Lee, H., 55
Lesaux, N. K., 21
Leu, D. J., 127
Lewis, C., 125
Lewis, J. P., 123
Linguistic dimension of reading, 13
Literacy
    complexity of, xix
    nature of, xiv–xv

McKeon, C. A., 21
McTighe, J., 5, 70, 125
Miller, N., 10, 80, 82, 98–102

Online reading, including families through, 113–15
Orwell, G., 48

Pacheco, J. E., 59
Padak, N. D., 21
Parent–teacher conferences, 2
Paris, S. G., 26
Participation
    of stakeholders in assessment, 105–18
    tool for describing, 96, 97
Paterson, K., 26
Pearson, P. D., 53
PLAN Reading Test, 119–20
Pollan, M., 45
Popham, W. J., 6, 15, 125
Postreading questions, 33, 40, 41, 42, 43
Power, B. M., 126
Preassessment, 54–58, 70–71, 72, 73, 74, 83, 84–85
    anticipation guide for, 95
    for online reading, 114, 115
    rubric for, 56, 84–85, 95, 114, 115
Prereading questions, 32–33, 37–40
Price, H. B., 126

Privott, J., 54
Professional learning communities (PLCs), participation in, 5–6
Prompting, 62

Rasinski, T. V., 21
Reading
    building knowledge base about, 12
    cognitive dimension of, 14
    connection with active thinking, 22
    development dimension of, 15
    linguistic dimension of, 13
    sociocultural dimension of, 14–15
Reading assessment
    administrators' demands on, 4, 108–10
    assessor role in, 8–11
    biology classroom example of, 45–48
    classroom-based, 7, 24–26
    dual goals of, 3
    feedback based on, 18
    gaps in, 4
    goal clarity in, 5, 11–15
    of growth, 4
    including families in, 113–15
    inquiry-based, 15–17
    liking as feature of, 59, 83
    optimal conditions for, 31–32
    as outgrowth of curriculum, 30–32
    planning of, 79
    as process, 18
    purpose of, 18–19
    stakeholder participation in, 105–8
    time investment required for, 27
    unprincipled, 9
Reading assessment tools, 31, 34–45, 54
    instructional responses and, 31
Reading comprehension, supporting, 53
Reading conferences, 115–18
Reading habits
    finding evidence of, 34, 35
    modeling of, 32
Reading skills, constrained versus unconstrained, 26
Reagan, R., 124
Record-keeping, 29–30
    tool for, 29
Response to Intervention (RTI), 24
Riddle Buly, M., 21
Riordan, R., 21
Royse, S., 10, 19–24, 26–28
    sticky notes activity of, 21–24
    think-aloud activity of, 26–28
Rupp, A. A., 21
Rutherford, M., 125

Schoenbach, R., 124
Scott, D. B., 25
Serafini, F., 15, 125
Seravallo, J., 126
Shakespeare, W., 90–93
Sharp, F., 10–11, 45–48, 80–82
Shepard, L. A., 7, 8, 15
Short, K., 15
Silva, C., 12

Sipe, R. B., 125
Slotnick, G., 11, 82–94
    reconsidering professional practice, 82–94
Sociocultural dimension of reading, 14–15
Sondheim, S., 105
Staff development, 81
Standardized assessment, 4, 19
    consequential validity of, 19
    deficiencies of, 20–21
Standards for the Assessment of Reading and Writing (SARW),
        Revised Edition (IRA–NCTE Joint Task Force on
        Assessment), xi–xxi
    assessment of language, xvi
    educators as learners, 81
    language of assessment, xvi–xviii
    learning of language, xv–xvi
    nature of assessment, xi–xiii
    nature of language, xiii–xiv
    nature of literacy, xiv–xv, 12
    standardized reading tests, 21
    standards, xviii–xxi
    teacher development in assessment, 112
    teacher knowledge, 12
Sticky note activity, 21–24
Students
    identifying strengths and weaknesses of, 27
    interests of, xviii
    participation in assessment process, 115–18
    responding to needs of, 21–24
    as stakeholders of investment, 18
Student versus content goal matrix, 83, 86
Student work, examining, 34–45
Summarizing
    guided instruction for, 61
    modeling process of, 61
    need for, 57–58

teaching and learning, 54–68
Summative assessment, 7
Swartz, R. J., 124

Teacher-facing questions, 69
Teachers
    anxieties of, 1–2
    collaborating with administrators on assessment, 108–10
    collaboration among, 110–13
    knowledge base of, 12
    as learners, 81
    maintaining autonomy of, 18
    modeling of reading habits by, 32
    as questioners, 94–97
    role in assessment, xviii
Teaching, effect of assessment on, 16–17
Text complexity, 58
Think-alouds, 26–28, 44, 79

Understanding by Design (Wiggins and McTighe), 5

Valencia, S. W., 21
Validity, construct versus consequential, 19, 20, 50

Waff, D., 125
Walsh, S., 27
Wiggins, G., 5, 70, 125
Wilfong, L. G., 21
Wolfe, M., 124
Wormser, R., 59, 61

Zelkha, S., 124
Zemelman, S., 123
"Zenning it," 83, 86, 93, 94
Zimmerman, S., 2

Author

Photo by Stacey Gross

Scott Filkins has worked as an educator in the Champaign Unit 4 schools in a variety of roles, including English teacher and department chair, reading teacher, instructional coach, and (currently) curriculum coordinator for English language arts and social studies, grades 6–12. He also codirects the University of Illinois Writing Project and is a doctoral student at Illinois in curriculum and instruction, with a focus on language and literacy and writing studies. Filkins worked at the National Council of Teachers of English on the ReadWriteThink project and currently serves on the ReadWriteThink Advisory Board for the International Reading Association. He lives in Urbana, Illinois, with his son, Colin.

This book was typeset in Jansen Text and BotonBQ by
Barbara Frazier.

Typefaces used on the cover include American Typewriter,
Frutiger Bold, Formata Light, and Formata Bold.

The book was printed on 60-lb. Recycled Offset paper by
Versa Press, Inc.